My Land Obsession

My Land Obsession

A Memoir

BULELWA MABASA

PICADOR AFRICA

First published in 2022 by Picador Africa
an imprint of Pan Macmillan South Africa
Private Bag X19, Northlands
Johannesburg
2116

www.panmacmillan.co.za

ISBN 978 1 77010 796 0
e-ISBN 978 1 77010 797 7

Text © 2022 Bulelwa Mabasa
Foreword © 2022 David Hertz

All rights reserved. No part of this publication may be reproduced, stored in or introduced into a retrieval system, or transmitted, in any form, or by any means (electronic, mechanical, photocopying, recording or otherwise), without the prior written permission of the publisher. Any person who does any unauthorised act in relation to this publication may be liable to criminal prosecution and civil claims for damages.

All photographs are from the author's personal collection.

Editing by Sally Hines
Proofreading by Sean Fraser
Design and layout by Triple M Design
Cover design by publicide
Author photograph by Jeremy Glyn (courtesy of Werksmans)

Contents

Foreword *by David Hertz* ix
Preface: A Life-Changing Moment on Our Family Vacation xi

Part 1:   Echoes of the Ancestors
 1   The Pillars 3
 2   511K 9
 3   Foundation 17
 4   Lights … Camera … Action! 19
 5   The Roots 24
 6   Mawe and Tata 31
 7   Lost Land 38
 8   Planted Seeds 42
 9   The Picket Fence 44
10   Tale and Babam 56
11   1283 63
12   Shades and Textures of the Land of My Birth 69

Part 2: A New Dawn
13   Blooming 85
14   The Greys within the Rainbow 91
15   Freedom 99
16   Enlightenment 101
17   The Law 110
18   A Glimpse into Practice 115

Part 3: On the Way to Becoming
19   A (Legal) Home 121
20   9/11 124
21   Signed Up 126
22   Tea Girl 130
23   Belonging 133
24   An Ambivalent Litigator 136
25   A Grandmother's Prayer 142
26   Arthur 146

Part 4: Heritage Meets Profession
27   A Mother is Born 151
28   Partnership 155
29   Independence 163
30   The Quest for Social Impact and Meaning 167
31   A Tale of Joy and Sorrow 170
32   Raising Children while Building a Law Practice 176
33   Crown of the Nation 179

Part 5: Of Land and Ancestors

34 A Land Reform Practice Takes Root 183
35 Rebuilding 187
36 Media Exposure 190
37 Saving a Sacred Seat for the Ancestors 192
38 Spirits Don't Cower 196
39 Recognising, Protecting and Supporting Indigenous Knowledge Systems 200
40 Not a Black or White Issue 204
41 Changing Tides and a Shift in Land Politics 208
42 Turning Points 212

Part 6: A Duty to Serve

43 The Struggle for Land Justice 219
44 An Ode to My Ancestors 231

Acknowledgements 236
About the Author 239

Foreword

'*Hamba uyoba sisbane MaDlamini.*'

'Go out there and light up the world,' the words articulated by Bulelwa's paternal grandmother, Sesi, on Bulelwa's graduation, in fact understate the impact that my co-director and close friend has on everyone her aura touches.

When Bulelwa asked me to pen the Foreword to her memoir, I had no appreciation of the enormity of the task and the privilege that was being accorded to me. As I paged through this book, I garnered a renewed appreciation of both the challenging road that Bulelwa has navigated and the incredible people who have guided her on her path to the pinnacle of the legal profession.

Her story is imbued with optimism and passion. It demonstrates the power of positivity and triumph against inequity and inequality.

To describe Bulelwa as lighting up the world perfectly describes her personality. She explodes onto the stage, dominates conversations and drives initiatives, invariably to a successful conclusion.

She is the epitome of a modern-day professional, perfectly

balancing the multifaceted challenges that she encounters. As important as the success of her career has been to her, so too is her bond as the matriarch of her magnificent family.

There remains a rift, some would say a chasm, between South Africans who constitute the so-called Rainbow Nation. It is a barrier that I have spent my life trying to break down. We have so much to offer each other, a fact that emerges with startling clarity from the kaleidoscope of experiences that burst forth from Bulelwa's life story.

Bulelwa is, to my mind, the best of a generation of South Africans who grew up during a time of great darkness and emerged into the light with an unquenchable desire to break down barriers and move forward as one. She is an integral member of the Werksmans family. Her team is an eclectic mix of the best South Africa has to offer. My life has been immeasurably enhanced by being part of hers.

On a personal note, my mother passed away earlier this month. She instilled in me a love of reading and writing, and I have, in consequence, kept a journal to record my life experiences for over two decades. Amongst my mother's greatest joys, aside from her family, was paging through each completed volume of my journal. I am saddened that she did not have the opportunity to read Bulelwa's story, as it is a manifestation of a life that has been well lived, which was my mother's credo.

David Hertz
Johannesburg
June 2022

Preface

A Life-Changing Moment on Our Family Vacation

It was in the Mueang Phuket District, in the resort town of Karon on the west coast of the island of Phuket, that the WhatsApp message dropped on my mobile phone. The text appeared as soon as we arrived at our hotel in Khao Lak. This was the last leg of our family vacation.

Even my beloved, forever cheerful, supportive, glass-half-full, happy-go-lucky husband Arthur was visibly drained, with both our girls, Ntsumi and Akani, eleven and seven, hanging beside him, and our boy Rixaka, who was five, clutched on my back.

We had just arrived from a day-long and insightful but tiring tour of the serene Karon Temple, the breathtaking and panoramic views of Karon Viewpoint overlooking the Andaman Sea, and the spiritually grounding and humbling Big Buddha.

It is virtually impossible for my husband and I to talk each other out of our shared sense of innate madness and a mutual insatiable taste for adventure. I am often tempted to believe the zodiac sign mumbo jumbo: me, the airy-fairy, open-minded and laid-back Libran consumed by his adventure-crazy, interesting and imaginative Archer spirit.

We should have known better than to wake up in the wee hours of the morning with three young kids for a tour that would last at least eight hours, when we were already two weeks into our Thailand escapade.

We had agreed early in our marriage that we would keep our spark alive by exploring at least one destination abroad not less than once a year – just the two of us. In fact, keeping each other's spirits young and vibrant was an essential part of the private vows we shared in earnest eight years prior in front of Reverend Dr Wesley Mabuza.

Our annual overseas pilgrimages soon morphed into at least one bi-annual trip taken in the latter part of the year, tagging the kids along with us. With both of us products of apartheid, born and bred in Soweto – albeit in distinctly different townships and eras – travel provided the perfect antidote to a life we had only imagined and had read about in books in our formative years.

We had been anticipating a meltdown from any one of the children on the tour as the scorching temperature reached unbearable proportions.

Our complexions had positively morphed from mild dark brown to midnight navy blue.

I spontaneously left Arthur with Ntsumi and Rixaka when I saw an ATM nearby. I was sure I was making a genius move, as I was concerned about the three little faces staring back at me with dehydration. My intention was to withdraw some cash and buy gallons

PREFACE

of water from the tired, unfriendly looking woman seated at her stall outside the temple. True to form, Akani tagged along with me.

The language at the ATM was Thai, with no English translation. I relied on my instincts and followed the prompts. When the ATM machine finally spat out the cash for me to pull out, I breathed a sigh of relief. I celebrated too soon.

What transpired was a struggle between my sweaty fingers and the ATM machine, which only managed to produce less than a third of the stack of cash and made it impossible for me to pull out the rest of the money. Attempts at trying to pull out the cash came to naught, and Akani's efforts came too late. The time was up, and I watched my ATM card being swallowed by the machine. It was too late to apologise to Akani as the swear word ejected itself out my mouth without warning.

By all accounts, a day that was dominated by the picturesque kaleidoscope of lush-green vegetation, the coral-blue ocean and arresting sunsets, and the spiritual fulfilment we had been exposed to on our tour degenerated into the infamous moment when Mommy lost the family bank card on the last leg of our vacation in Thailand.

Feeling depleted and deflated, and frantically trying to contact the bank back in South Africa upon arrival at the hotel, I noticed the text sent earlier, which was from an unknown number but was clearly from home.

This was not just any text. It read: '*Mrs Mabasa, the Office of the Presidency has been trying to reach you. Kindly indicate when you may become available to take a call from His Excellency President Cyril Ramaphosa.*'

As we never do when travelling abroad, we were not on a

roaming service. The WhatsApp message must have landed hours before, perhaps while I was being the toss that lost the bank card.

I removed the cold, damp towel offered by the friendly and ever-smiling hotel host to cool me down, which I had placed around my neck. I wiped my sandy sunglasses and the screen of my mobile phone – in case I was hallucinating.

I knew instinctively that the one and only reason that the president of my country would seek me out, or even bother to have a conversation with me, would be none other than the subject that had occupied my mind and soul for as long as I can remember. I felt a rush coupled with the urgency and anxiety of having missed the one phone call that could alter and enrich the course of my career.

Here I was in the middle of my family vacation, two months before my 39th birthday, surrounded by my young family, almost 10 000 kilometres away from the country of my birth, right there in the middle of the hotel lobby, carrying backpacks, sticky toys, fatigued from the full day of touring and dressed in a sarong and bathing suit. My life was about to be catapulted from a singular, insular career trajectory to one that was to shoulder the hopes and dreams of my fellow countrymen.

Once the initial shock had subsided, a series of comedic and panicked episodes followed. Arthur eased the moment by whisking our fidgety and fussy kids to the hotel villa, while I ran to find the best spot with Wi-Fi connection.

Back home, the usual Khemese girls' melodrama had ensued in earnest. My four younger sisters, Naniwe, Fuziswa, Ntombizone and Nomfundo, had thoroughly immersed themselves into the project – 'How to make sure the president's call is returned'. They

PREFACE

devised a plan to at least make sure a call was made to the president's office on my behalf so that I did not in any way lose this once-in-a-lifetime opportunity. They are a resourceful, wonderful, brilliant and hilarious lot. Our father coined us 'Gangsters' Paradise', denoting our collective strength as a force and our ability to rally behind a purpose and each other. True to their Type-A personalities, and results-driven and assertive natures, they made sure a message was communicated to the president's office to convey my acceptance to form part of a ten-member panel to advise the president on a new policy on land reform in South Africa. Although this was my moment, it never really is about the individual with our shared sisterhood.

My mind momentarily flashed back to 2001. I had celebrated my 21st birthday three months prior. My paternal grandmother and namesake, Sesi, had handed me a R50 note and a white candle on the day of my graduation celebration so that I could, in her words, 'Go out there and light up the world.' *'Hamba uyoba sisbane MaDlamini.'*

It felt like a lifelong prayer was answered. The day our family vacation was potentially ruined by that text was also the day I was chosen by the president of my country to add my voice and mind to review and potentially resolve the land question, which has been front and centre since the formation of the Republic itself.

The time had come. I felt ready, hungry and affirmed. At the end of a rather eventful day, I managed to find a moment of solace at the resort. Just before sunset, the imposing trees, the sounds of the ocean and the chirping of the birds all pointed me to the echoes of my ancestors. In that moment, I was Bulelwa, the granddaughter of the Khemeses and the Mametses. Not a mother, not a wife, not a partner of a law firm, not a big sister. I took in the sunset rays landing gleefully on my back. I curled my legs up, pressing my chin against my knees. I envisioned Mawe's words: 'Go out there and light up the world.' My mind also saw my maternal grandmother Mmapapo's praise-singing at my undergrad graduation. To me, this was not merely an intellectual exercise. It was a spiritual call. I knew it. I had no doubt. I placed my feet into the warm pool, taking a dip in honour of my ancestors.

PART 1

Echoes of the Ancestors

1

The Pillars

I hear the day I was born was joyous. Glorious, actually. A rainy day, to be precise. And as Xhosa people would have it, rain is considered a reliable signifier of acquiescence directly from the ancestors. Nothing beats the approval of the ancestors, or rather this is what I deduced as a child, having grown up in a household of ardent, practising Christian Methodists who equally practised African spirituality. I was ensconced in this dual reality, which is considered a paradox to some and an abomination to many. To me, it was not until much later in life that I learned that popular sentiment had it that one either had to be Christian or believe in ancestral worship – not both. To date, I have still not quite grasped or been convinced of the supposed contradiction.

I was told that the falling of rain on the day of my birth sprung an idea in some family members' minds that I should be named Nomvula (the Rain Queen), which I thought was ludicrous the first time I heard it and far too literal. Rain has a deep symbolic meaning for Xhosa people and throughout southern African spiritual practices. Rain is significant not only for its environmental role but equally so as a symbol of abundance and cleansing in the material and spiritual sense.

The day of my birth was joyous because Mawe and Tata's eldest son, Reuben Malusi Khemese, known to many as Ompie and to me and my sisters as Babam, had, together with my mother, Pamela 'Tiny' Masopeng Khemese (née Mametse), produced their first child and daughter.

This was a few weeks before Babam (on cello), his younger brother Sandile (on first violin), Joshua Thelele (on viola) and Koloane Mantu (on second violin) – four young black men from Soweto – were invited to perform at Haddo House in Aberdeen in Scotland for Lady Aberdeen.

This once-in-a-lifetime opportunity was marred by the reality and impact of the apartheid regime on the immediate lives of these four men from Soweto.

The day of my birth must have been a joyous and welcome deviation from plans falling flat on the ground in Babam's life. When Babam and the quartet travelled to Aberdeen, they were reminded in the most hurtful way that they were from South Africa – the land of oppression and dispossession. They were not allowed to perform after all, managing only to jam here and there with local musicians on the side. Sanctions against South Africa were taking root in Europe and the United States. Sweden formally passed legislation prohibiting the formation of any new companies in South Africa. The US not only reduced its military staff based in Pretoria, but it also prohibited the granting of loans to the South African government. The dream of an international career was not to be – at least not yet. Babam becoming a father for the first time also marked a sense of triumph of dreams over apartheid.

My connection to Babam is not only biological; it is also spiritual as much as it is cultural. In Xhosa culture, the first paternal female grandchild is often but not always named after the paternal grandmother. In my case, I inherited Mawe's name 'Sesi' as my middle name. She, too, was the eldest female daughter, just like me. I spent most of my life not owning or even appreciating or recognising the name, owing to childish shallowness. I would have preferred a name like Petunia, Julia or Gloria then. Those were the names that had popular appeal and a sophisticated ring to them. The girls with those names were some of the prettiest around. Almost every black person in my generation and the ones before either had to or elected to have a Christian or English name. I did not cherish the name Sesi because it appeared quite glib and superficial to me. It denotes eldest daughter. Eldest sister. Exceedingly literal. Nevertheless, I did not truly appreciate just how profoundly I would subconsciously take on and wear the mantle and weight of that name, neither did I value both its burden and glory, all at the same time.

Born in the township of Meadowlands in Soweto and spending the first seven years of my formative life there, I devoured every tale and anecdote I had the fortune of being told, or rather overheard. Nothing could retard my sense of curiosity, whether this was what I had heard or read. From my aunties, uncles, neighbours and even friends, all that I routinely heard was '*ukrelekrele lomntwana*'. Their eyes sparkled at the sight of a little girl who was often buried in a book and could read and write fluently in isiXhosa and English long before her peers. Always the youngest in the class, I was three years old when I started the first grade. In retrospect, I grew up affirmed. I knew I mattered. My world rendered me valid. I was decidedly bright in their eyes. I believed them. The validity of my ancestry would act as a fortress against any type of enemy. At least, this is what I was made to believe. I was sure of the sturdy nature of the shoulders that I stood on.

All I had known and needed to know until that point was that I was of Xhosa origin, born into the Khemese family, which hails from the loud and proud clan of the Dlaminis, o Jama ka Sjadu, originally from the former Transkei. This was by virtue of my father's paternal blood line. Our paternal heritage was carried through to us by my orphaned grandfather, Nkwenkwe Elliott Themba Khemese, fondly known to me and to everyone else who knew him as Tata.

I had met my maternal great-grandmother, Belina Matseke, once with my mother in her rural home village of Marapyane. Her face was covered in a multitude of ridge-like wrinkles, leaving indisputable evidence of a full and convincing life. I was initially afraid of her. She sat on the grey, icy, concrete floor in the main bedroom, with her legs neatly curled behind her like a pretzel. She was small and ancient. Something about her body language signalled someone who was done. Done with everything that she was here to do. Her face was glued to the ground, not keen to make eye contact. This was the first and last time I was in her physical presence. What seems to have to stuck in my six-year-old mind was her amber, oval-shaped, thick-beaded necklace and her tired spirit, mirrored in her begotten, blue-grey eyes. She wore matching beaded earrings, a clear statement of a woman who was not deterred by age to tend to her looks and beauty.

There was an indestructible bond between my mother and Belina

THE PILLARS

that was formed when my mother was uprooted from her home in the village of Marapyane to Masobe to care and look after her blind grandmother. To Belina, my mother was more than a granddaughter. She was the one of six other grandchildren who spent her most impressionable years of life being her eyes and helping Belina to run a shebeen that sold traditional beer out of her home. But this was not a one-way street. My mother often shared with me the magnitude of love and lessons she gained from Belina.

Belina served in my mother's life, alive and posthumously, as her north star. Her lighthouse.

I had met and known my paternal great-grandfather, the towering Sekolo Masote, whose distinct physical feature was, outside of his tall, imposing, commanding presence, his half pinky finger, which was apparently the result of an unfortunate accident while working in a butchery in his youth. He had a rough, chesty voice, his back was bent in a semi-circle and he was reliant on his walking stick. His teeth had all fallen out and he was quick to laugh, often pointing at his subject with his interesting finger. His wife Johanna's maiden surname was Fakude. Of Swati heritage, she enjoyed her beer and had a sense of humour that was riddled with metaphors in her younger days; this was later replaced by a sharp tongue and a strict disposition.

Interestingly, both my maternal and paternal grandmothers, Elizabeth Mmapapo Mametse (née Matseke) and Winnie Sesi Khemese (née Masote) were the eldest daughters in their respective families, both born of the Kgabo Bakgatla clan, with roots in the village of Masobe. Both their fathers were descendants of the Matseke clan.

My maternal grandfather, Rapereng Michael Mametse, was born in a rural village known as Uitreg. He was one of seven siblings. Rapereng was a stern disciplinarian, leaving little to no room for aimless banter. Not a beneficiary of the finest education by any means, he had the foresight and knowledge of the importance of education in the lives of his seven children. This largely illiterate man produced two nurses, four teachers and a lawyer, ensuring that all his children firmly internalised the fact that it was only through education that the cycle of poverty would be dismantled.

Knowing who I was, who I came from and the heritage of my ancestors, I was enough. I felt anchored. I was surrounded.

2

511K

511K Ipiva Street in Meadowlands Zone 4 was the address of the home in which I spent my first seven years of life. I remember it as much more than a physical address – more of an imprint, part of my DNA. These years shaped me in unimaginable ways and left a lasting impression on me. Crucially, Ipiva has no meaning at all, or rather cannot be translated into any of the South African languages, at least not from what I could gather.

This happened a lot when the Afrikaner-led regime would make up and string words and syllables together that have no meaning or origin in any African language, with the sole purpose of ascribing to them an 'African flavour'. I was always intrigued about the meaning and genesis of things. Ipiva Street consisted of two opposite rows of small and crammed houses that almost resembled a railway line, or railway coaches separated by either a thin wall or a barbed-wire fence, depending on the household's level of economic muscle.

Everyone knew everyone by name and surname, young and old. I only learned later of the existence of the 'picket-fence family' (none of which existed in Ipiva Street, with one or two exceptions).

The size of the homes ranged from two to five rooms, yet each home was inhabited by three and sometimes four generations. Grandparents were overwhelmingly the primary caregivers and often the breadwinners.

Facing the street from the right end was a timber yard, which sold coal and timber – both essential commodities on the brutally cold winter nights when every family was reliant on coal-fired stoves to keep the houses warm. It was only much later in life that I realised that the overwhelming smell of smoke at dusk was not a natural condition but was interwoven with the architecture of apartheid. The government of the day did not humanise black lives, such that we were not connected to the electricity grid for at least the first three years of my life.

I did not know that the combination of the smell of smoke and moms calling out their children's names at the top of their voices in an elongated tone at sunset was something peculiar to life in Meadowlands. The coal-fired stove was the centrepiece, akin to the Western dinner table, where families gathered at the end of the day. For those without the stove, there was *imbawula*, a fire made in a metal container with makeshift protruding holes, which was useful as much as it was deadly. Many died from smoke inhalation if it was not taken outside overnight. Some of us were able to tell the tale, judging from burn wounds and scars on my body, no thanks to the Ellis-branded stove in Mawe's kitchen.

The sounds of Ipiva Street were colourful, varied and textured. From the corner house labelled 'Jericho', due to the incessant arguments and physical fights that sometimes led to stabbings among family members, to the sound of children competing over *ibhathi*, or an uncle showing off a new set of speakers and blaring Lionel Ritchie's 'All Night Long' or Chicco Twala's 'We Miss You Manelo', a catchy hit song that lamented the absence and incarceration of Nelson Mandela. At this point, many, including me, had not seen any images of the man, and the mere mention of his name triggered terror in the adults and sheer mystery for the young ones. Given the ban of black political parties and prisoners, it would have been a punishable offence if the song failed to contain the decoy of Manelo instead of Mandela. Music carried us. It was us. The aspirations, hopes, dreams, failures, disappointments and even heartbreak were expressed in song and dance.

Children of working parents would be asleep when their mothers and fathers quietly and hurriedly left home before dawn, and, if lucky, they would see them again just before bedtime. Many parents worked as domestic workers in the white suburbs, 'garden boys' and factory workers, most managing to come home only on weekends or perhaps fortnightly. For those who were mineworkers, they only went home once a year during the December holidays.

The community and the streets replaced the role of parents. Each child belonged not only to their immediate family but also to the community. The teens with raging hormones would hide discreetly at street corners while making out. They knew that if MaMkhize, who was not related to them, saw them, she had full authority to chase them away and even to separate them. This did not stop at the communal disciplining of children, but it also applied to food security. It was not a strange phenomenon to open the door in response to a knock without first knowing who was behind it. Sometimes, it was a child from next door sent by the elders, holding an empty mug to ask for some sugar. Or it could be the regular vendor walking house to house selling merchandise, ranging from clothing to sweets and even furniture items. Being sent on errands to deliver messages or myriad things was part and parcel of being a child in Meadowlands.

Any family that was hosting a wedding or funeral knew that the women of the street would rally, clad in pinafores and doeks and carrying a knife, ready to peel and cook the night before – burning the midnight oil in preparation for the next day.

Sounds and sights of the religious community were prominent in the form of African Zionists in green-and-blue attire holding sticks or the Apostles in their red-and-white berets. Sundays were especially vibrant. The food we ate on a Sunday was different – and special. Our plates boasted seven colours from all the food groups. It was not just the food – it was the fact that everyone was always dressed in their Sunday best. Even the man who was known to be the clumsiest dresser made an effort. After church, every household would blast their favourite music, some even placing the speakers at the entrance of the gate, facing the street. For those lucky enough to have cars, Sundays were also the days that turned yards into car washes.

It was the confluence of exhilarating energy that connected me deeply with the black condition, without having the vocabulary for it. I knew I loved it for all its flaws. Despite this period taking place at the height of the apartheid regime, which was determined to dehumanise, emasculate and erase the dignity and relevance of black people, my childhood memories seemed to point towards a people who were expressly decisive about finding joy in the midst of the doom and gloom.

The separation of races by biology, geography, opportunity, and economic and social status on a macro level was not enough for the apartheid regime. It was important that the separatist development carried itself through to the colour of each household's stoep or porch. The apartheid regime's obsession with division and difference resulted in Zulu-speaking households having black-painted stoeps, the Tsonga- and Venda-speaking people would mostly have green stoeps. You cannot make this up, but this was as real and as ridiculous as apartheid got. The level of respect and dignity one attributed to a neighbour was dependent on the colour of their stoep.

Of course, the might of the apartheid regime did not end in its mindful execution, it was propelled by the fact that African people themselves not only subconsciously bought into it but also endorsed it and in many ways even became its ambassadors. I say this because I grew up not necessarily being told but seeing and sensing, for example, that Tsonga-speaking people somewhat belonged at the bottom end of the African 'tribal' food chain, if ever there was one. I could discern this by judging how many kids would be seen frequenting the Tsonga-speaking households. Usually there were none.

The children from Tsonga-speaking households would play in their own yards and rarely mixed with the rest of the kids in the neighbourhood. They seldom truly assimilated into the community. They were fluent in isiZulu or Sesotho, while the isiZulu and isiXhosa speakers felt no compulsion to learn Xitsonga. As expected, and as perhaps as nature would have it, the deadly combination of fear and ignorance resulted in inevitable mystical stories about Tsonga people that were not based on the truth. The Tsongas signified the height and depth of blackness – they tended to be blue-black – the kind of black that was not desired and was considered ugly. They were more often than not clad in their traditional, bright colours in *michekas* and *xibelanis*, walked barefoot and kept to themselves. They were natural traders – sure to be found on street corners selling vegetables and fruit. They were the furthest people from the ultimate dream of proximity to whiteness. Not too much blame can be attributed to the aspiration of whiteness because, as life turned out, it carried with it both opportunity and fortune.

There was a Tsonga-speaking household right opposite 511K. The mysterious house was occupied by a certain Mr Chauke, and no one else. He hardly interacted with anyone. He was a middle-aged, dark-skinned, short and stocky recluse. The broken windows were patched with old newspapers and torn book covers. Through the broken windows, one saw only darkness. To make matters worse, not only was he a Tsonga man, he was also a traditional healer, in particular, an *inyanga*. Being an *inyanga* catapulted him several notches into the world of shameful mysticism and ridicule. In the eyes of devout Christians and the formally educated, traditional healers fall within the category of heathens and outcasts.

Mr Chauke's tiny, three-roomed house looked incredibly spooky. What he got up to was anyone's guess. What I found strange though is that through the darkness, Mr Chauke consulted and saw hordes of people, who were obviously either shamed or shameful about openly seeking his services.

Our next-door neighbours to the left were also a Tsonga-speaking family. Unlike Mr Chauke's home, this house had several inhabitants. Both parents, the brothers Josefa and Tomas, and the sisters Dlaweleni and Johanna and their children lived in the three-roomed house. There was always a level of warm familiarity with this family, but the thin concrete wall separating the two households also ensured an element of safe distance and 'difference'.

I had never entered their yard and neither did they enter ours, although no one ever verbalised us being forbidden from doing so. Johanna, the younger of the sisters, would often be heard yelling and hurling insults at her elderly mother, especially at night. Her mother was a scrawny, quiet, squint-eyed and wrinkly faced woman who made a living from making *ntsu*. Every night, we would hear from Mawe and Tata's bedroom a loud, rhythmic sound and banging on the ground. This sounded like an iron-made structure banging onto cement ground. According to Mawe, the matriarch at our neighbour's house was making *ntsu*, a form of dried or moist tobacco, inhaled from the nose or put inside the lower lip, cheek or gum. *Ntsu* was and continues to be a common feature in almost every household in the black townships, young and old, male and female. *Ntsu* is also colloquially known as 'black cocaine'. It is often a standard feature seen on graves of loved ones when communicating with the ancestors.

To the right of our home was the Nkosi family, who originated from Swaziland. Babu Nkosi was always courteous, dignified and neatly dressed. The relationship with the Nkosis was cordial. Things took a sour turn when Babu Nkosi passed away. It turned out that the woman we thought was his wife was not his only wife. In fact, she was what is called *umfazi we phepha*. This is a woman married to a man in civil law and not traditionally. The migrant labour system, being a dual, unnatural and untenable system, resulted in many men who worked in the cities entering into relationships with women they met in the city, when, back home in the rural areas, they were in fact married traditionally. This scenario played itself out in front of my eyes when Babu Nkosi's traditional wife laid claim to his house in Meadowlands as the rightful owner, and when we had known only of Mam'Nkosi, the city wife.

By the time I was born, the 1950 Group Areas Act had been in existence for 29 years, initially under the leadership of former Prime Minister Daniel Malan. In a weird but telling way, this piece of legislation would determine the lens through which I viewed and experienced life. It impacted on the trajectory of thousands of families and contributed to the demise of many family structures. It made way for forced removals without warning or bargaining, where black people were forcibly removed from occupying urban areas that were earmarked for white residential and commercial use and development. I was born at the height and might of racial segregation and the denial of basic human rights for black people.

The township of Meadowlands was significant in its own right. It was one of the first products of the Group Areas Act. When Africans were violently evicted from Sophiatown, which was a relatively multiracial suburb, one of the first destinations would be the township of Meadowlands.

The name Malan rolled off Mawe's tongue, laced with melancholy and utter disdain. Little did I know that Malan was not just a sole entity and a pariah; he was, in fact, the face of a determined apartheid state and machinery to ensure that the existence of many generations of black people stayed repressed, irrelevant and erased from history.

3

Foundation

Kwa-Phalo Primary School was within walking distance from our home at 511K. It was hardly a kilometre walk. A pathway had eventually emerged along the weedy, unkept and neglected shrubs on the route to school. Children from our street walked down the road and turned either left or right just before the makeshift soccer grounds. The children turning right were in a green-and-white uniform and making their way to Kwa-Phalo, a Xhosa-medium school. To the left was the pathway leading to Mpumalanga Primary School, a Zulu-medium school, with those children dressed in a navy-and-yellow uniform. Dividing the two pathways was a rubbish dump and behind it the soccer pitch, with the typical, orange-tinged grounds and tiny brown stones that announced themselves when they unceremoniously pierced your feet. The walks to school were made up of dribs and drabs of groups, and they were never a lonely exercise.

Water rarely came out of the only tap at the school. The top part of the tap mechanism was often mysteriously removed. God forbid if I was ever in need of going to the bathroom. The mental preparation that preceded that visit was disproportionate to the mere natural act of relieving oneself. It was extremely dark in there – pitch black, in fact – and one was overcome by the thick stench of stale urine and faeces, even before you entered. The walls in the toilet were full of graffiti made from dry faeces, marking pens and pencils, with a glimpse of what was once a coat of olive-green paint. One would find every type of profanity, curse and blasphemous material smeared on the walls, including the names of other children. Walking into the bathroom engulfed me with fear. When winters were particularly bitter and there was no water, Principal Lujabe would often ring the bell and dismiss classes for the day, much to the euphoria of the children. This was not a rare occurrence.

I had to make certain that when the school bell rang, I was already inside the school premises, or there would be hell to pay, and there was. In all the years spent at Kwa-Phalo, the windows were permanently broken. The brokenness of the windows became part and parcel of the school aesthetic. I grew blind to them, except during the frosty winters. The shivering was not only brought about by the cold. Entering the school gates evoked the same reaction. Every single time. The closer I drew to the school gate, the louder the heartbeats, louder than my little heart could bear.

4

Lights ... Camera ... Action!

I could never have predicted that by 1983, at the age of four, I would be one of the first black children starring in one of the first television children's programmes, *Ikhaya Labantwana*, an educational show that could be likened to *Sesame Street*. There was a man on Ipiva Street who was known to many as 'Major'. He loved the arts, particularly performing and acting. He would gather the older teenagers from the street and arrange dance-offs, skits and many other cultural activities. Music, dance and song were undoubtedly an outlet and a response to the repression that lingered in the underbelly of the community.

I hear that I was quite talkative and bright-eyed as a four-year-old. This led to Major noticing me when he was involved in the production of the new children's programme. He liked my inquisitive nature, and this culminated in me spending a year or so playing a lead role in this show. This was probably the best time of my young life. I quickly bonded with my on-screen parents. The cast was very close to one other. I had to learn my lines written in isiXhosa, and I loved the allure of the camera. I came alive. I knew then the feeling of what happens inside me when I did something that agreed with my soul.

Being fetched from 511K at 4 am every second day meant I missed out on school, much to my relief and delight. We would either shoot shows in the studio, then known as Heyns Films, in Halfway House, or we would shoot on-site at different locations. My co-star was Mongezi Mbele, whose mother later became the headmistress of Kwa-Phalo. Her name was Nomalizo Mbele, and she was the maestro of the Kwa-Phalo school choir, which was the jewel of the school.

The trips that ranked prominently in my memory were the ones to the zoo, the theatre, libraries, the airport, museums and simply just going to different locations for the TV programme. This was the first window of opportunity that opened my soul. The experience was more valuable than the education I was receiving in the actual classroom. I also had an on-screen grandmother who was always smiling; but none of these actors felt like my actual parents and grandmother. The privilege, fortune, opportunity and exposure of being on the television show did not diminish the familiarity and warmth of my real-life family.

Ikhaya Labantwana was also significant for reasons that are less than noble. As smart as I was at the age of three or four, I used to come home from shooting and revert to my first love. My bottle. My bottle with Nestlé baby milk in it. I would curl up with Mawe on her green leather couch and drink my bottle. Until I couldn't any more. One day, while watching myself in one of the episodes and merrily drinking my milk, Mawe made a threat that crumbled my world. She stood in the passageway facing me and matter-of-factly said: '*Wonke umhlaba ukujongile pha ku TV. Xa ungayeki le bhotile … ndizakubiza o cameraman bazokubona xa usela le bhotile.*'

I shuddered when I thought about Mawe's threat to call the camera crew to film me drinking my beloved bottle at the ripe age of four. And so, *Ikhaya Labantwana* represented the moment I subconsciously in the mind of a four-year-old learned that what you do in private must be something you ought to be proud of if revealed out there.

My mother often remarked about how I would doze off in boredom when I was at school and not shooting. When the teacher was trying her best to keep me stimulated about colours and shapes, I told her: '*The boredom is unbearable, the only thing to do is sleep.*' I was at Thabisile Primary School for pre-prep in Diepkloof township in Soweto. It made sense that I was enrolled at a school in Diepkloof, given that my mother was a nursing sister at the nearby Diepkloof Clinic, as it made the commute between Meadowlands and work easier. My mother and I travelled by taxi from Meadowlands to the pre-prep. The trips we made to school and back were most pleasurable. I had her all to myself. This was a rare treasure. She was stunning. Her lips were thick, and her eyes were small and slanted downwards when she laughed or smiled. Her nurses' uniform was starched pure white and worn with absolute pride. Her petite body was shapely, and her waist was minute. Her skin was tender. To me, her natural scent was a combination of fresh rose petals and burnt charcoal. She wore brown nurses' shoes, and walking beside her, with her firmly holding my hand, always made me feel safe. I loved her permed Afro. As a child, I thought that her deep and scratchy voice was a little embarrassing at times and the way she ground her teeth incessantly, especially when she was silently cleaning the house, which was often. Time with my mother gave me a sense of security. She was herself. Unique. Special and like no other.

I lived for the trips with my mother. I was in complete awe of her, taking in her work ethic and how she showed up for her calling. I had not quite connected the link between her love for midwifery and public healthcare and making money for a living. To me, it always seemed that she was sent to Earth to be the superhero that she was. As such, it dawned on me very early in my life that her calling and purpose in life as a health worker did not compete with the fact that she was my mother too. She did not compartmentalise her life. When it was time for her to be at work, I did not feel short-changed in any way. She was just my mother who also had her role to play in the world. She had a clear and unmistakable sense of purpose. She was sure about each stride she took. She was someone I wanted to become. She was gentle and tough, all at the same time.

Those trips were our love language away from the activity of the boisterous home at 511K. She often told me that I did most of the talking, and she chuckled in amazement. Actually, it was probably me doing most of the asking. She said she could not lull my curiosity, and often she would sometimes feel like literally shutting my mouth with her hands, especially when we were inside a taxi, although she never actually restrained me in any way. When a strange man I did not know would innocently strike up a conversation with her, I would pipe up at the top of my voice: '*Tale angithi wena ushadile? Ushade no Babam! u Babam usebenza e South African*

LIGHTS ... CAMERA ... ACTION!

Breweries and unemoto, akahambi nge taxi uhamba nge "Cressida".' She was in a constant state of embarrassment or sheer disbelief about my lack of a verbal filter.

These trips also became ominous in another way. My appearance on the television show, which was aired daily, became a living nightmare. Suddenly, I would be walking with my mother on the streets and a sea of children, who were strangers, and even adults would flock towards me, eliciting monstrous heart palpitations and a desire for the world to open up and swallow me.

My very first day at primary school at Kwa-Phalo was disappointing to say the least. The hope I had of some semblance of anonymity and blending into the crowd without anyone recognising me did not come to be. A group of older kids came towards me, taking a bet on whether I was in fact the girl from *Ikhaya Labantwana*. Others downright teased me about why my hair was always in pigtails on the show and that I was too dark-skinned to be on television. I wished I could be invisible whenever I was in public. I developed an intense self-consciousness and felt lonelier and lonelier with each day that passed at school. It was clear I did not belong. I yearned for the same level of freedom I had witnessed in other children. Later, I was lucky enough to form a bond with two of the smartest girls in the class: Pretty Munyai and Paula Mathonsi. In them, I finally found people who also did not enjoy it when others made a noise in class and who really wanted to engage with the material we were being taught. It was like we were hungry lions being fed after a long lacuna.

5

The Roots

By the standards of the day, our home at 511K was one of the bigger ones, which boasted a concrete, plastered wall as its facade, three fair-sized bedrooms, a bathroom with an in-built bath and a toilet, a decent-sized kitchen and a dining room. It was a privilege to have a bathroom that was part of the house structure, as most other houses merely had a toilet built outside the house and no bath or sink. Many families opted to build 'backrooms' in their modest backyards, and these were largely rented out to third parties for extra income amid the mass densification that was taking place in the black townships. But Tata chose a fruit, vegetable and flower garden for his backyard. His green fingers resulted in our home being surrounded by various fruit trees – apricots, grapes and figs. Our backyard was lush and entrancing. The vegetable patch had a spread of pumpkins, tomatoes, beetroot, garlic and various herbs. The garlic often ended up either in our throats as one of Mawe's homemade remedies for a sore throat or it was used in the *spuit* for a digestive cleanse.

Whenever Tata worked in the garden, which was daily, for what seemed like hours on end, he was always dressed in his long-sleeved, starched white shirts with rolled-up sleeves and formal trousers. Tata held on firmly to his sense of dignity; he almost insisted on it in a world set to dehumanise and emasculate him. I always wondered how he never managed to get himself dirty. At this point, Tata was already on pension. He decidedly poured himself into the work of his hands and heart. But, more importantly, what he could not do with his own children – which was to give his undivided time and attention, given his all-encompassing churchly and choral leadership duties – he more than made up for with his grandchildren.

If Tata was not working in the garden, he was reading or writing hymns, softly and quietly humming the melodies, rocking his body side to side on the white bunk stool as he constantly corrected his manuscript. His persistent, phlegmy cough became part of him. It seemed it never left him. I wondered whether the years working underground as a mineworker at Crown Mines had anything to do with it. If he was not reading, writing and singing, he was reading the Bible. This was intriguing for someone who did not undergo any formal musical training and who taught himself how to read and write. He was not reading the Bible glibly. He was subsumed by it. His Bible was rather battered, tattered and littered with highlights and underlined verses. When he was not immersed in reading the scriptures, he was surrounded by no less than twenty children between the ages of six and sixteen, including me and my younger cousins. He formed what was called The Band of Hope, which he and Mawe ran together. He had built a form of a shed with benches made from boulders in the backyard, and they would teach us how to read hymns and sing in tune. Tata was largely patient but intolerant of any one of us who sang even slightly out of tune. I was once or twice the recipient of the infamous slap on the wrist: once when my emerging and excitable singing voice went into unceremonious vocal overdrive, and another time when I prolonged a joke whose time had long come and gone, resulting in me distracting another child.

Tata was a disciplinarian who suffered no fools. He embodied the kind of self-discipline and natural and unforced righteousness that made you want to pursue perfection. You knew you simply had to behave. The Band of Hope was, in essence, my introduction to the principles and values of Christianity and an affinity with music, particularly singing. During the December school holidays, we would prepare for Christmas skits and choral competitions with groups from other parts of Johannesburg and beyond. This time coincided with the colourful vibrancy and palpable exuberance of the Khemese household, when my father's sisters – Nonceba, Stella and Vuyelwa – would be seen hurriedly but meticulously preparing their hairstyles, and ironing shirts, dresses and church choir attires for the choral festivals nationwide, under Tata's direction and leadership. There were occasions when my father and his brothers took over the baton from Tata, with notable wins and performances by the Zone 3 Methodist Church Choir. In many instances, Mawe and each of her daughters, my aunts, were lead soprano and alto soloists in various competitions.

Breaking into song was commonplace in this household, and it never really required an elegant schedule. It could have been triggered by one of the aunts shining the stoep, and, soon enough, it would turn into an impromptu choral festival in the middle of

THE ROOTS

Mawe's kitchen. There were other occasions, of course, of planned and focused choir practices. In these moments, I observed Tata playing his role as a professional maestro, which carried with it an air of unmistakable seriousness that made it palpably glaring that the stakes were high. When Tata was conducting the choir or his wife and children, he remained a consummate professional.

I later researched the source and genesis of the concept of The Band of Hope and found that it originated in Leeds in the United Kingdom in 1847. It was part of Methodism in the UK and Ireland. Influenced by the temperance movement, it forbade the consumption of alcohol and advocated for the awareness of its dangers. When Tata and Mawe hosted their 'IOTT' temperance sessions at home, I was particularly curious about the friends clad in red-and-blue regalia and sashes, who gathered in the dining room with Bibles in hand. IOTT is an abbreviation for Independent Order of True Templars, but the brothers and sisters of the movement colloquially referred to it as 'I ONLY TAKE TEA'.

Everyone in Meadowlands knew that alcohol was forbidden at 511K. For Tata, his hatred for alcohol was not simply a result of his religious inclination. He narrated to me how he had witnessed fellow mineworkers squander their week's wages on what he considered to be an apartheid drug. This was not because they did not know any better, but because the apartheid regime was so intent on thwarting the development of the black man that he said on every corner a shebeen was carefully planted, such that many men simply did not and could not resist the lure of the apartheid drug.

During this time, Naniwe, my sister who was two years younger than me, my cousins, Zithulele and Tsami, and I were the only grandchildren in the home. We were later joined by Monde and Thembi, whose mother was Kuli, my father's cousin. Before that, the four of us would sleep on the concrete floor in my grandparents' bedroom. We got accustomed to sleeping in musty-smelling blankets. I can still smell the muggy dust under the bed, as my night view consisted of old, dusty pairs of shoes. I remember the vivid smell of Vicks VapoRub, which I often used to rub on Mawe's back. It became part of our night ritual. I took great pride in fisting, rubbing, clasping and clutching through her loose skin on her back, as if I was moulding and stretching dough in the process of baking.

Both Mawe and Tata had an affinity for all things earthly and earthy – from Mawe only using herbal and plant-based remedies for most, if not all, our childhood ailments, to being known as the local 'midwife', who would be called upon to assist women who gave birth at home. She did this for many households in the neighbourhood.

Mawe was not a formally trained midwife, at least not in the Western sense. I later learned that she took up a first-aid course of sorts and worked at the then J.G. Strijdom Hospital. I gather that her life's purpose and interests collided in an uncanny fashion, centred on healing: healing of the body and of the spirit. I was subconsciously being dunked into respecting and honouring indigenous African knowledge systems and African spirituality, which was absent throughout my life in formal education. I also recognised that Africanism concerns itself with being, more than it does with seeking.

I hardly recall visiting a medical doctor, let alone a paediatrician in my formative years, notwithstanding the fact that my mother was a formally trained nursing sister and midwife. There was never a time when I thought that Western medicine was antithetical to traditional medicine, and my mother knew exactly how to navigate these seemingly contradictory philosophies. She gave Mawe the space to take over and knew instinctively when it was time for me to be taken to St John's Eye Hospital for my spring catarrh, which was a rare allergic eye condition I grew up with, and when it was time for me to be taken to a traditional healer for my low muscle tone. It did not occur to me until later in life that these were philosophies that society deemed divergent and irreconcilable.

Mawe knew exactly which herbal plant to use for any childhood ailments. She lived for her flowers and plants and called them by their botanical names. When our throats hurt, she would use a squeaky clean, white cotton cloth dunked in a syrup-tasting pink liquid. The unseemly part of that process was when she would force my mouth wide open, squeezing my cheeks on both sides to reach my throat. Mawe and my mother were a lethal pair. They plotted and colluded. They defied the notion of a typically terrible mother and daughter-in-law relationship. They were allies at best and, at worst, co-conspirators. One of their show-stopping, mother-of-all remedies, the most feared, was the *spuit*. After Christmas and New Year, a week before schools would open, my cousins and I would be lined up in a queue outside the toilet and wait our turn for the dreaded *spuit*.

A *spuit* is best described as a syringe or an instrument that can withdraw or inject liquids into the anus. This was done primarily to cleanse the digestive system after the festive season, which always included gemmer (ginger beer), countless scones, biscuits, jelly, custard and trifle. The *spuit* usually contained water with crushed or grated garlic.

Mawe was soft-spoken, with gentle but tough wrinkly hands and a tender spirit. She also had an intense intolerance for nonsense. Even the kind of nonsense that came naturally from a child. You very much never wanted to be in Mawe's bad books. Some of the moments I treasure to this day are when she and Tata would wake up in the wee hours of the morning to watch local and US-based boxing matches on their television in their bedroom. They would let us watch with them. To say they were committed fans of the sport would be an understatement. Tata would often tease her about how he only went for her because of her ugly looks and that he felt sorry for her because he figured no guy would ever find her attractive. According to him, he pitied her and did her a huge favour. This would invariably set her off into a frenzy of endless and unstoppable high-pitched giggles, and we would join in the raucous laughter. Of course, Mawe was the opposite of ugly, especially in her prime. This much was abundantly clear from their wedding picture taken in 1951. She, sporting a short Afro, with velvet-like smooth and perfect skin and an arresting smile, and Tata, a tall, handsome man standing upright and confident.

6

Mawe and Tata

My grandparents shaped my formative years in ways that leave me inspired. They were real-life examples of the first people I knew and loved who directly bore the brunt of a regime that was intent on separating the country by race. This regime systematically and purposefully crafted a society on the false notion that white supremacy was not only a natural reality but also a biblical necessity that became woven into the psychological, sociological and economic layers of the lives of black Africans. I have always thought that white supremacy did as much damage to white people as it did to black people, because it dished out to them generations of underserved, inexplicable and gratuitous forms of privilege that resulted in a society riddled with inequality and pain. It also bequeathed white South Africans an intense ignorance and a complete lack of insight or knowledge that deprived them of knowing not only the drudgery of being a black person living in South Africa but also the gems and pearls that resulted in countless black folks claiming joy and triumph, despite it all.

Tata grew up in the rural Transkei in Zimbane. Not much has

been documented about his village. He was an older brother to his only sibling, his younger sister, Notizi. They were orphaned early in their lives in a very remote part of the Transkei. Legend has it that they were raised by their grandmother, their late mother's sisters and kind neighbours in the village who took them in. One such family were the Fincas. Little to nothing is known about their biological father. Tata and Notizi belonged to the Dlamini clan, o Jama Ka Sjadu. Like thousands of other youths, Tata was forced to escape the poverty and dearth in rural Transkei in pursuit of a better and possibly more illustrious life in urban Johannesburg, the City of Gold, full of promise and wonder.

Later in life, the boy from the Transkei would graduate from being a boy to a well-respected patriarch and leader in his immediate family and his wider community. In my eyes, his mature age did not take anything away from his stoic nature. He was my grandfather after all. He was anything but weak or frail. Quite the opposite. The only signifier of his age was his silver soft mane and his wrinkles whenever he smiled or laughed heartily, which was most of the time. You would also notice his age when he gave you the disapproving eye, or the quiet look of pride, or even the impatience of the unconscious knowledge that forever is not forever. Tata was a strikingly good-looking man, with eyes that slanted downwards when he smiled and laughed. He was very fair in complexion, which often led to questions about his genealogy.

My early memory of Tata was that of a present, dignified patriarch, who worked for a major electrical wholesaler by day, and by night was a respectable, active and present husband, father and grandfather. At home, he displayed the same ease standing in front of the kitchen sink washing dishes quietly and delicately as he did waking up before we all did to cook us brown sour porridge. He had a job that paid the bills, but he also had a full life that allowed him to live out his purpose – as a leader in the community, a Methodist man of God, a preacher, and an innately talented chorister and choirmaster. Although he did not say so, there is no doubt in my mind that his day job would have somewhat diminished the essence of who he was and who he was meant to be. His hands were always crafting, whether it was working in the garden in our backyard or building and making wooden chairs and garden furniture. He was as much a craftsman as he was an artist. More than that, he was a man who crafted his own sense of reality – one that would insist on his human dignity and a sense of being beyond his day job and the trappings of a cruel system intent on dehumanising him. He was somehow able to break away from the shackles of the limits of apartheid that were set to reduce him to a mere labourer. At the same time, who knows what the lengths and breadth of his influence would have been beyond his community had he lived in a different time and space?

I was fortunate enough to have witnessed Tata in action in various roles. On the pulpit whenever he preached, and as part of the congregation, I rarely understood or internalised the Word. It always went above my head, as it was far too metaphorical for my developing young mind. By contrast, the elderly ladies sitting near me would often utter 'Hallelujah', and some would perspire incessantly, leading to a trance-like state and some collapsing in the process. The small building would sometimes feel like it was caving in, in response to the spirit of God that contained the place like a glove. Unlike some of the other preachers, whenever it was Tata's turn, you could hear a pin drop. You could sense the intensity and fire in the room. Legend also had it that Tata was the sought-after preacher during the much-anticipated Seven Words service during Easter. The Easter services took place at Zone 7 Methodist Church about 5 kilometres from the Zone 3 parish. Zone 7 is a bigger circuit parish. If the Zone 3 church services were unbearably long, the Zone 7 services were even longer. The heat was invariably difficult to bear. No matter how early you arrived, children would always have to give up their seats for the gogos. What I understood clearly though is that each preacher was assigned one of the Seven Words and, true to form, Tata would always feature in the programme as one of the preachers who would be assigned to preach about one of the Words. Tata preached in isiXhosa and sometimes dabbled in Sesotho translations. One Word I vividly remember him preaching was the Word *Kugqityiwe*. It is finished. Those who subscribe to the Christian faith will understand that this was the last Word that Jesus Christ uttered on the cross. On these occasions, we had to arrive with my mother several hours before the commencement of the service. Although I did not have the vocabulary then, I was able to dwell in a room full of mainly adults, praying incessantly about young men who were targeted and taken away by apartheid forces, or young women who were jack-rolled by local gangsters. Religion and politics were inherently intertwined. Tata had the congregation's full attention. I knew then that he was an important man. He would also usher in the choir at the beginning of the service and lead them out again at the end. The services were far too long, interchanging between standing up and sitting down. God remained mysterious. I often wondered at what point He would deliver miracles and relieve these adults from their desperate pleas.

Tata shared with me the tale of how one day he and Mawe were unexpectedly and cruelly uprooted without any prior notice from the home they had built (or rather tried to build) and grown to love in Sophiatown. In their words, Sophiatown was a confluence of South Africa's bustling multicultural and multiracial diversity, with African, Indian, Chinese and Coloured neighbours living in proximity and relative harmony. Not many tales are told of a time in South Africa when racial division was not a dominant feature.

Mawe and Tata's dreams of a bright future were shattered when apartheid policemen one day descended in Casspirs, demolishing houses and seizing personal belongings, forcibly removing them and their young children from their home to a makeshift area a few hundred metres from a graveyard. This place was Jabulani. It seems that Jabulani was a temporary holding place, prior to their ultimate forced move to Meadowlands. A Zulu word meaning 'be happy', Jabulani would be a far cry from happiness, having heard stories from my father of what appeared to him and his siblings as a haunted place in the middle of nowhere.

When he arrived in Johannesburg, Tata was one of the young recruits sought or lured by the apartheid regime from the former homelands during the surge in the gold-mining period in the Witwatersrand. He would be one of many hundreds and thousands of young black men who were used as cheap labour to work in the mines and enable the migrant labour system. Essentially, the black family structure was destroyed by a system that uprooted fathers and husbands from their homes when they were moved to mining towns and housed in what were called 'hostels', which were akin to male barracks. These men would only be allowed to go home to their wives and children once a year. The migrant labour system doubtlessly served to eat away at and erode the fabric of the African family. Even in modern-day South Africa, the absent father phenomenon continues to bedevil the life experience of many South Africans.

There were things that struck a chord with me when Tata shared stories of his life as a mineworker. Among them were the inhumane and undignified body searches these men had to endure to satisfy their bosses that no gold was stolen. He related this tale in jest mainly but in graphic terms, telling me of how they would be stripped naked and then asked to separate their buttocks, line by line, in the interests of building an economy that would ensure that generations of black people would remain on its periphery.

Despite all the odds, Tata managed to attain major accolades in his life as a well-respected and renowned community leader, a co-founder of the Mzimvubu School, which doubled as a community church, and the Zone 3 Methodist Church and choir, which was not only revered for its excellence but also for being awarded many trophies in national competitions across the country. In a way, music and the stage were his saving grace — these were the moments that redeemed him from the plight of apartheid. The orphaned little boy from the Transkei, who yearned to become a man of the cloth and to preach the word of God, had lived a lifetime walking and dwelling in His light and purpose.

When Mawe was eighteen, she was spotted in the choir where she sang lead soprano by one of the missionary scouts and offered a scholarship to become an opera singer in the UK. Her voice, a natural and pitch-perfect soprano, was the second thing that Tata noticed about her; the first was her beauty. She was born on the wrong side of history. And, being a girl, her parents simply scoffed at the idea of their eldest daughter being whisked away to faraway foreign lands, and they expressed shock and horror at the preposterous suggestion of a girl who was coming of age focusing on anything other than creating her own family. Her dreams of being a famous opera singer may not have come to bear, but, as fate would have it, her womb would birth three sons who became ambassadors for African classical music worldwide and she would live to see that day. The dream of a world-renowned opera singer later manifested in her own sons in the most remarkable ways. When nature wants what it wants, it does not stop until its call is answered.

7

Lost Land

It is impossible to speak of Meadowlands without reference to the catchy marabi protest song 'Meadowlands Mielieland', written by Nancy Jacobs. The upbeat and vibey nature of the song is rather misleading, as the song is a lament of lost dreams, lost hope and loss of a sense of place for thousands of black families in 1955. The song was a direct response to the forced removals, with lyrical content in Fanakalo, a folk language that has a mixture of Zulu, Afrikaans, English and Sesotho.

The removal of Mawe and Tata from Sophiatown was not only a physical displacement and dispossession; it went much deeper than that. When the Casspirs and bulldozers arrived to remove them from their land, their sense of being, dignity and heritage was erased, which was so interconnected and merged in the land itself.

I was born in a township that was rooted and birthed in many losses, landlessness, pain, defeat and racial segregation.

Perhaps even more symbolic was the cultural practice shared with me by Mawe that all her children and grandchildren's umbilical cord stumps, once they had fallen off, were buried in the soil in our backyard at 511K. I was not spared from the custom that kept me eternally connected to the land of my ancestors, and which was guaranteed to keep me anchored, curious, intrigued, pained and also healed by the land question in South Africa.

Meadowlands had an impact on my life, as my parents, Ompie and Tiny Khemese, lived at my grandparents' home for the first seven years of their marriage. It was very common (and still is) for children to remain in the 'family home', even after they graduate into adulthood and marriage. As a result, most households were occupied by grandparents, parents and grandchildren, and also often included cousins, aunts and uncles.

The idea of the family home even extended to the need for many families to build backyard rooms to make provision for the growing household. Everyone knew who 'belonged' where. Everyone knew which house belonged to the Khemeses. There were rarely conversations, conflicts or disputes about 'ownership' of the various houses. At worst, I would overhear Mawe lament about rental payments that were due to KwaMuhle. I would later learn that KwaMuhle was the Home Affairs Department, to which local households were expected to pay monthly rentals.

My childhood at 511K is best described as vibrant, joyous, musical, love-filled, warm and empowering. Our home was a typical matchbox-style house, consisting of three bedrooms, one bathroom, a kitchen and a dining room. A lounge was added later in the 1990s. The main bedroom was occupied by Mawe and Tata; the second bedroom was occupied by my parents; and the third bedroom was occupied by my three aunts. The dining room was a dining room by day and converted into a makeshift bedroom by night, where my boy cousins and uncles slept under the round mahogany table.

There was never an inkling that we lacked anything. The fact that we never had birthday presents or toys did not register as poverty. Sleeping on the floor did not appear to signal an overcrowded home. In fact, the feeling I ascribe to growing up in this house is that of abundance: abundance because my uncle Sandile would lift me to the top of the fridge with the stereo next to me, singing along at maximum volume to the sounds of Al Jarreau. My uncle Thamsanqa loved to spend time with me and tell me stories about his youthful shenanigans with girlfriends. My aunt Nonceba would plait my hair on weekends, and my aunt Vuyelwa would constantly shower me with words of affirmation and imprint on me the love of beautiful garments and immaculate grooming. Being dark-skinned was celebrated in this household. My mother would make me repeat to myself each time she bathed me and gently moisturised my dark skin: 'I'm Black and Beautiful,' echoing the black pride movement in the US. These seemingly purposeless mechanical chants landed as a personal attachment. They went to the core of my being.

Perhaps another reason that I may have missed the fact that we did not have a lot in a material sense is because I had witnessed Mawe every supper time dishing up for more than twenty people at a time, some of whom I later learned were not blood relatives. Each day consisted of either choir practice, a women's *manyano* prayer session, a children's Band of Hope drama practice, which often included my grandparents and all six of their children – Stella, Malusi, Sandile, Nonceba, Thami and Vuyelwa – who were all at some point or another talented and leading choristers.

Both Mawe and Tata made marriage seem like a harmonious melody, filled with beautiful crescendos that made up an orchestra, which was enjoyed by all who had the luxury of finding themselves in their company. Joy, abundance and immense love underpinned my formative years.

8

Planted Seeds

A conversation I had with my father as a five-year-old planted a seed in me. I was intrigued and drawn by a painting that hung on the wall in the passageway between the bathroom and the dining room at 511K.

It was a painting of a striking, chocolate-skinned, round-faced, tearful young girl, with piercing almond-shaped eyes and curly hair. In her, I saw myself. Like me, she had big eyes, a long forehead that led to her flat and broad nose and a thick mane on her head. Her lips were full, but her expression was hopeless and masked by visible pain. The painting was signed 'Verna' at the bottom.

Despite my best endeavours, I have not been able to locate the identity of the artist. My conversation with my father went something like this: '*Babam, why is she crying and why are her clothes torn?*' Babam responded with distant eyes: '*She is crying because her land was taken away from her.*' This conversation and the answer given by my father would occupy and haunt my entire being. It was prophetic. I would spend the next 35 years of my life subconsciously seeking the answer to the reason why this young black girl, who looked a lot like me, could possess such sadness. Why was I living in a world where land could be taken away from you without any remedy or consequence?

This painting and conversation would play louder and louder than the dominant classical and choral music and the joyous and raucous laughter that was the backdrop and atmosphere of life in the Khemese household.

I knew then that there was an underlying layer of sadness, despair and hopelessness beneath the joy and laughter. I would spend the rest of my professional and personal life seeking the answer to the question I asked my father at the age of five. My father had unknowingly planted a mental seed that morphed in ways I could never have imagined.

I grew up picturing and visualising myself – over and over again – standing in front of a courtroom, defending the rights and interests of black landlessness in that painting.

9

The Picket Fence

Naniwe and I despised moving away from living with our beloved Mawe and Tata. It was towards the end of 1985.

South Africa was burning. Literally and figuratively. The stories of teenage boys disappearing were commonplace. My youngest aunt Vuyelwa – like hundreds and thousands of youths in the black townships – had to be moved to one of the more politically stable former TBVC (Transkei, Bophuthatswana, Venda and Ciskei) states in order to access uninterrupted education. She was sent to the Transkei. Schools in black urban areas were places of danger. The politics of the country had reached boiling point, and the National Party government had responded by imposing a national state of emergency. The country was on a precipice.

My acting gig on *Ikhaya Labantwana* at Heyns Films had come to an end. I loved being in front of the camera – it came naturally to me – although I despised what it meant for life outside of it. When Major informed Babam at the end of the season of the upcoming television shows that I was earmarked for, I was ecstatic. I also wanted to be a ballerina. None of this was to be, and I was shattered. Babam had decided. I begged Babam to allow me to continue with life as a TV star. True to form, he did not relent. My pleas fell on deaf ears. '*You are a bright child with potential. You cannot continue with this TV thing and be a part-time scholar. You need to focus on school completely. The TV thing ends now.*'

My resentment grew every day. Unable to hide my feelings of disappointment, I reminded them at every given opportunity that I was well aware of the fact that they purchased the new house with *my* money from *Ikhaya Labantwana*. Their shamed faces gave me internal joy and a sense of retribution.

Nani was four and I was six. There was no electricity for the first few months in our new home. It was devoid of the effervescent energy and warm affability that we were so accustomed to living with Mawe and Tata. To me, this was a bad decision. The street would always end up in a muddy flood because there was clearly no adequate drainage, and our house was a stone's throw away from a smelly wetland with stagnant water that stank up the area. Although the finishes of the house were newer and better than 511K, the kitchen was much smaller. It took us a while before we considered 1283 Naledi Ext 2 a 'home'. We would always wonder about and yearn for our friends who filled up our yard at 511K, practising choral songs or me playing teacher and writing behind Tata's storage shed, which was my makeshift chalkboard where I gathered my friends – me being the self-appointed teacher and them always obliging me.

Spending less and less time with Mawe and Tata left a gaping hole in my heart. I jumped at every opportunity we had to visit 511K. We would conspire with Mawe and Tata, pretending to be fast asleep when our father came to fetch us after work to leave for 1283. As Babam entered Mawe and Tata's bedroom, Nani and I would be under the covers on the floor dead quiet, and we would overhear Mawe saying: '*Kudala belele, bayeke uzabafumana ngomso, Ompie.*' We would not utter a word until we heard my father start his car and drive away. At this point, we made an absolute racket, squealing in delight and jumping onto Mawe and Tata's bed until we really fell asleep.

We loved that we had a bedroom we could call our own in the new home, but it was still not 511K. The arrival of our baby sister Fuziswa in January 1986 provided some comfort for our longing for life in Meadowlands. In fact, it signalled a nuclear, focused family that we never had before. Although our parents lived with us in Meadowlands, they were preoccupied with their working lives as one would expect of a couple in their mid- to late twenties with three little girls, determined to chart their own path in life.

The arrival of Fuziswa immediately turned the house into a home. I lived for the time to come home from school just to smell her. It was the first time I came to know the smell of a baby, and I planted my nose deeply into her black, thick, curly hair that looked naturally moisturised. She had a deep gaze, even as a baby, as if she would penetrate the depths of your soul. I found a beloved new doll, except it was human. She was the perfect baby, releasing a soft groan when hungry or when her nappy needed a change: a baby who never made a fuss. I quickly became a deputy mother, eagerly learning how to soak the cotton nappies and helping to hang them on the washing line with pride. In my eyes, baby Fuziswa solidified the beginning of a fully fledged Tiny and Ompie family set-up.

THE PICKET FENCE

The house at 1283 gave my parents their first opportunity of being figures of authority in their own lives. In Meadowlands, Mawe and Tata were unmistakably the drivers and captains.

At 1283, the face and shape of a family as I had known it had completely changed. There was none of the eclectic energy of strangers coming and going. We missed the hearty meals that Mawe made, particularly her bony soups in the winter, and the sour brown porridge that Tata made in the crisp mornings.

Life at 1283 gave me my first taste of being a so-called nuclear family and particularly the practical meaning of being the eldest child. My familial responsibility was heightened by the need for me to take much more responsibility in the daily functioning of our home. I needed to step up in many respects, and I did. This was our picket-fence family.

My mother, whom we called 'Tale' (pronounced 'Tuh-leh') and my father Babam were 32 and 33 years old respectively when we moved into 1283.

This was their season to cultivate and craft a life they wanted us to have in the future. They worked hard. The long hours clearly took a toll. They did not need to mention their struggles. I saw and heard them: from Babam walking to the train station to buy meat, from the street vendors we would witness, from him and Tale opening drawers to gather some more coins to come up with R10 and returning with chicken gizzards or chicken livers wrapped in white paper. I soon learned that the cost of a live chicken was cheaper than the one from the butchery. This was my mother's specialty. It looked gruesome to me when she beheaded the live chicken. What I found utterly scary and intriguing at the same time was how immediately afterwards the chicken's beheaded body would continue to skip from one spot to another, even in its headless state.

I watched my mother silently and intently slaughter the chicken while grinding her teeth. I grew accustomed to my mother's incessant grinding of teeth; it was what I heard when she was deep in thought, silent or especially worried. Usually this happened as she scrubbed the floors or washed the clothes with all her might, as if her life depended on it. After the chicken was beheaded, she placed it in a large bowl, poured boiling water over it and left it to soak overnight. In the morning, she would wake up at dawn and pluck the feathers until there was no trace. She then boiled the chicken from morning until afternoon. It struck me how much time and labour it took for our parents to put food on the table. She was pretty much the same way when she was preparing *mala wa mogodu* (tripe), especially as she rinsed away the waste from the intestines. *'The aim is not to kill the taste. Don't clean the intestines to the point of sterilising them.'*

My mother's Kgatla, rural upbringing kept her rooted and firmly grounded. Being a professional woman and living in the city took nothing away from her authentic self, her humanity and her strong sense of purpose.

Although we needed to be on our best behaviour at 511K, we felt free to express ourselves, and we had countless light and silly moments with Mawe and Tata. It was vastly different at 1283. Our parents always seemed to be in a rush. A rush for survival. They did not have the same aura of calm and being in the moment that our grandparents had. I found myself increasingly straddling the hard line of discipline and decorum that my father commanded and the high sense of responsibility that my mother clearly needed.

Babam worked for South African Breweries as a supervisor. He arrived at home every evening without sight of a smile on his face. He was heavy-handed and had the aura of someone who was highly dissatisfied with life. Nani and I were terrified of him and found him rather insufferable. Whenever we heard his car pull up into the makeshift garage, Nani and I would frantically ensure that we picked up toys, packed away shoes and made sure no dirty dishes were in the sink. Tale was also part of the mission to make sure Babam did not explode the moment he entered the lounge. It was impossible to predict what or who would set him off on an emotional outburst. The dishes could be sparkling, but a double electric plug could be missing from his bedroom. One time, it was raining cats and dogs, and, upon hearing the doorbell, I asked who was behind the door like we were taught to. I experienced the wrath of his temper when he barged in angrily and yelled that I should have simply opened the door, given the bad weather conditions. I felt like an imbecile. I quivered at the knees and felt terror run through every part of me. I ran to my room, hid behind the door and wept. He had that effect on me. He was someone who left no room for error. I always fell short of his impossible standards. At least, that is how I felt.

Babam spent most of his evenings in his bedroom on his own. He would sit in the bedroom chair, often in the company of his gigantic glass of beer, a Hansa Pilsner or a Castle. Contemplative. Silent. He was dark-skinned, his face often had an oily glisten, his physique was plump, and his hairline was receding on the sides. With a perfect set of pearly whites, he laughed hard when he laughed. When he was in a good mood, his laughter was always preceded by a mischievous smile. His humour was dominated almost always by poking fun at someone else. It often irritated my mother – and me. His humour had an air of teasing, not always in a welcoming sense. The palms of his hands were a tobacco-stained colour, and he had stocky fingers. He walked with great intent, broad-shouldered and upright.

It was clear to me that he had a rhythmic and melodic tune that lived internally in his soul. As outwardly sad as he may have been, the music in him kept him joyous inside. I say this because whenever he walked along the pathways of our home, he would always be whistling one tune or another. He would strum his fingers against the walls. There was a fire that raged in the depth of his soul.

He devoured classics by Bach, Haydn, Mendelssohn, Beethoven, Vivaldi, Mozart, Brahms and others. He was extremely single-minded about the music he consumed, never dabbling in other genres until later in his life.

Babam had a coercive approach to making us do what he wanted. There was no negotiation, and I dared not voice my misgivings. I did not even know that I was allowed to have any. His passion and unadulterated love for classical music was quite frankly foreign to me. I stared at the LPs of old white men in blond wigs and wondered what it was that swallowed Babam into a world that sailed him into a spiritual trance, with his right eyebrow rising along with the crescendo of the piece. He came alive not only in his listening session but also when he held and sat behind his cello. It was as if the instrument itself was designed with him in mind. He was his cello and his cello was him. He practised his cello for hours and hours after work. I would even hear the melodies deep in my sleep.

I had wished he played more, but his travel from 1283 to Isando where he earned his living must have been gruelling – both in mind and in spirit. His commute was easily 130 kilometres per day. He must have been desperate to infuse his love for classical music in us, perhaps combined with his need to keep us off the streets, such that he one day informed Nani and I that we would be attending violin lessons at the University of the Witwatersrand every Saturday. This was both sad and good news. It was sad because we detested learning the instrument, but we hated his brand of strict and intimidating teaching methods more, never knowing when he would hurl: '*You idiot! Play that note again until it is precisely in tune!*' At least he would no longer be our teacher.

The journey of being misfits escalated to new heights when our shameful violin playing had to be witnessed outside the four corners of our home. It was bad enough that Nani and I would overhear the delighted shrieks of our peers playing outside, much to our envy. Daily violin practice was compulsory in our home. If we failed to put in hours of practice, Babam had an uncanny ability to notice it, even on the first note. It got to a point where our disinterest was overshadowed by our fear of Babam. Because Babam had the gift of vision, he quickly decided he would give up the gig of being violin teacher and outsource it to someone else.

We travelled by taxi from 1283 to Wits University. The trip was roughly 20 kilometres and involved taking two and sometimes three taxis before we arrived at Wits. These trips shaped my mind and perspective. I became aware of the face of hopelessness and helplessness during our commutes. The desperation of the mama on the sidewalk selling sweets and vegetables struck me. The face of the man who seemed idle on the side of the road with a 'looking for job' cardboard sign gripped me. The small children in soaked nappies with flies and traces of oil and pap residue on their faces, who lurked and ran around in taxi ranks, concerned me. And yet here we were, carrying black violin cases, off to spend hours with a Canadian virtuoso who would teach us to play an instrument I cared little about. I could not unsee the levels of difference. The trips to Wits that were meant to teach us how to play the violin solidified my innate eye and heart for what is just and what is not. To my adult mind, these were the stitches that were woven in my heart.

Carrying those funny-shaped black cases on our backs attracted the most unwanted and tormenting type of attention from taxi drivers and fellow commuters. Nobody seemed to know what this instrument was. It did not help that I was as dark as charcoal, as thin as a rake, with an abnormally elongated neck and had a clumsy posture. Some taxi drivers would insist we put our 'tennis rackets' under the seats, and others teased and taunted us about being guitar players.

By the time we climbed the concrete stairs of the imposing Wits School of Music, we were fatigued by the anxiety of the consequences of having failed to practise, or not progressing from playing first to third position. It must have been a combination of fear and disinterest that caused a complete refusal of our brains to penetrate any violin-related material. It was a sad state of affairs, especially for our world-renowned new teacher, Professor Walter Mony.

THE PICKET FENCE

We were blissfully ignorant of his illustrious accomplishments and globally decorated biography, including him once being a member of the London Philharmonic Orchestra. We were already jaded, and nothing and no one could be paid enough for us to give the violin a fair chance. The privilege and fortune of spending every Saturday with this fine gentleman for several years was lost on five kids from Soweto. Our cousin Zithulele and two other children from Soweto came in and out with us every Saturday – all of us barely making notable progress on the instrument. None of this deterred Professor Mony's determination, love and willingness to continue pouring his heart into teaching us. His gentle manner and kindness were completely antithetical to how Babam had taught us. On one occasion, Professor Mony innocently blurted out a comment about my physique. *'You have the most graceful, beautiful neck – perfect for a budding violinist.'* So, it was possible that I was not a ghastly looking creature after all.

Night-time at 1283 mainly consisted of me being forced to listen to the news in English in an effort to improve my understanding and vocabulary, and sometimes it involved reading English newspapers. This was not the worst of Babam's demands. It piqued my genuine love for reading, current affairs and politics. I was immersed in hearing and reading about the fall of the Berlin Wall. I was drawn into the intricacies of the Yugoslav Wars and the 'Talks about Talks' in South Africa, which led to the negotiations between the African National Congress (ANC) and the National Party. This was in preparation for the transition of the country from a white minority state to a constitutional democracy. South Africa would usher in the first democratically elected president in its history. I watched in earnest the news images of Cyril Ramaphosa and Roelf Meyer, wishing that I could be a fly on the wall during those negotiations. Perhaps my obsession should not have been what it was, given my tender age, but nothing and no one could divert my genuine interest.

When Babam and I and were glued to the newspapers, with me often reading to him, or the television, our minds were locked in a dance. In these moments, my terror of him was overridden by the exhilaration of the time we were living in. Although I may not have had the appropriate vocabulary for it, one thing was certain – the world was shifting, and I was alive to see it all.

Babam fed my thirst in very deliberate ways. I understood that the colonisation of Africa by European countries was, in essence, the stripping away of a sense of dignity, a sense of being and a sense of place for generations of Africans. The uprisings and struggles in the fight against colonialism in African nations were firmly rooted in the struggle for land. Right there in my own home, I was unknowingly experiencing the school of social justice, law and politics, with Babam as my enabler and driver.

I buried myself in Wa Thiong'o's *Petals of Blood*, Serote's *To Every Birth Its Blood*, Achebe's *Things Fall Apart* and Biko's *I Write What I Like*. These were some of the masterpieces that liberated my mind and gave colour and texture to everything I had suspected was wrong with my world. Many truths were woven into those fictitious characters, plots, histories and storylines. I romanticised and idolised those living at the height of colonialism in Africa, be it in Kenya, South Africa or Nigeria.

THE PICKET FENCE

In the literature, I found the kind of black excellence and pride that I could not readily identify in my immediate setting. In words of fiction, I was able to connect the dots. There was real life, made up mainly of consistent chores and trying not to upset my father, and then there was the blissful escape I found in books.

10

Tale and Babam

On paper, Babam was statistically one of the lucky few boys to grow up with both his parents, who were in a loving relationship and were relatively unscathed from the social and economic devastation that swept through the black experience. But this was only superficial. He had trouble in mainstream school, where he repeated various grades.

In those days, there was no care or need to assess the mental, emotional or even psychological ability of black children. The education system was not designed to produce black physicians, intellectuals, astronauts or philosophers. It was designed for black children to grow up as fodder for unskilled and semi-skilled labour into an economy that was created to serve the interests of the white minority. Babam was a casualty of an education system that had no meaningful place for a black child.

To rub salt into the wound, he had the misfortune of being placed in the hands of teachers who simply did not care enough about his academic progression. At some point, he spoke openly to us about being the designated messenger to run teachers' errands in town for various reasons and skipping many classes, much to his relief. Some of the teachers were known to consume alcohol during class, which was disguised in mugs. This also made him the ideal candidate for routine, gruesome corporal punishment. He increasingly became a recluse and kept to himself. He endured deep levels of self-doubt and low self-esteem.

His story, however, took a different turn when his mother Sesi's youngest brother, Michael Masote, decided to start the first black orchestra and string ensemble school in Soweto at the famous Uncle Tom's Hall. Mawe and Tata enrolled him and his brothers to join the music school in 1967. My father had finally found his place and a voice. This was when he discovered his talent and natural flair for the violin and the cello. His uncle had become an igniter and an illuminator of what was possible.

By April 1987, my parents' fourth daughter Ntombizone (a Xhosa name that literally means 'four daughters') was born just fifteen months after Fuziswa was born. Fuziswa instantly became Babam's baby. She brought to our home a sense of family and vulnerability that was hidden deep under the heap of discipline and good behaviour that shaped the face of our family. This was when Babam's gentler and softer side emerged. He was besotted with Fuziswa. He must have decided that he would ease Tale's load and became remarkably present in Fuzi's rearing. He took her everywhere he went and even got himself and Fuzi matching outfits.

Zone, by contrast, was a high-needs baby. She was pretty, with chubby cheeks and Tale's characteristic small eyes. She clung to Tale for dear life and was not as easy in personality and temperament as Fuzi was. She spent the first months of her life permanently perched on Tale's lap, and she was sensitive and not easily sociable. Born with a club foot, I witnessed Babam and Tale rally around and take Zone to regular physiotherapy. Our narrow passageway between the two bedrooms and kitchen was the area where my baby sister, clad in black ankle boots, was assisted to make her one foot straight.

Within one year of having moved into 1283, our parents had four daughters and two bedrooms, one of which was shared among the four girls and Mma Mokobodi – our long-serving, Pedi-speaking, highly efficient and effective helper. The quick growth of our family demanded from us all a new way of being.

Both Babam and Tale cemented themselves as part and parcel of the small community. They endeared themselves to their neighbours, even forming part of a community stokvel. This also meant that we made friends with our neighbours. Some close bonds were formed, and 1283 became bearable after all. But still, I knew that there was always a lingering feeling that much more was in store for me. There was a life after 1283. I felt it. I wanted it. I was going to find it. Or rather, it would need to find me.

This period was dominated by the incessant washing of dishes, scrubbing of floors, sweeping of carpets, and dusting of cupboards and cabinets. My ability to clean the house ranked high on the measurement stakes and I did not disappoint. My mother was sure to remind me at every turn, 'You are the mother of my children.' I nobly took on this mammoth responsibility. I owned it. I lived it. In the ecosystem of the Tiny and Ompie household, I was in charge. I was my mother's co-pilot. My mother relied on me, and I devoured the role of being needed, of being useful to the most important woman in my life. She, too, did not waste a moment to brag to anyone who cared to listen about what a treasure I was.

Even at 1283, Tale was Tale to all. This name originated from Nani's inability to pronounce her nickname 'Tiny', and it stuck. She was indeed petite, with a small frame and a height of less than 1.55 metres. She wore her heart on her sleeve; the doors to her home were as open as her heart. Many loved her openly, visibly and loudly, because she invited that kind of magnanimous love, paired with her famous warm embrace. Her presence was undoubtedly ubiquitous. Tale had seemed rather scarce at 511K. During our formative years, she was building and crafting her career as a nursing sister, a midwife, a student and, ultimately, a nursing college executive.

Born and bred in the rural village of Marapyane, she was the third child of Ntate and Mme. She expressed how fond she was of her father Michael and how he was fond of her – leading her three sisters and three brothers to the conclusion that she was her father's firm favourite.

In the migrant labour system, black men were forced to live and work in the cities, while their wives and children were left behind in the rural villages. Virtually no black family was unscathed by this system. Migrant labour took away my mother's father from Marapyane to work in the capital of the country in Pretoria, over 100 kilometres away. Ntate, their father – as Tale never failed to mention – was harsh and strict.

I had long come to the conclusion that the inhumane conditions of the time subjected black people to figures with no nuance or complexity, but people with a singular purpose nonetheless, which was to try as hard as possible to shake the chains of a cruel system.

To survive. To live from day to day. To try to not get killed. The precarious nature of the time must have seeped into the joy of parenting. It is difficult to imagine a touchy-feely and syrupy love when our forefathers' struggle for survival and to live hung in the balance.

Ntate worked as a 'garden boy' for an Afrikaans-speaking family in Pretoria, managing only to be with his wife and children over the December holidays. For the rest of the year, back in Marapyane, his wife Mmapapo kept the home fires burning and assumed the strength and order that required both a mother and a father. By all accounts, Mmapapo played her role with aplomb and never complained about raising seven children on her own. Like Zone, she too had a club foot, which caused a permanent limp. Unlike Zone, she did not have the benefit of medical attention to rectify the condition.

Mmapapo was blessed with a beautiful arithmetic brain. She could memorise family and friends' telephone numbers off by heart until late into her eighties. I often heard how she was top of her class at school. She was a woman of sharp intellect and quick wit. She exemplified to me why receiving formal education on its own cannot be considered a measure of intelligence and wisdom. She was a product of her time and denied an opportunity to continue with her high-school education, given that as the eldest girl in her family she was expected to leave school, seek work to help support her family, look after her two younger sisters, and eventually be married off.

In a twisted way, both my grandmothers' wombs bore children who were implanted with their talents and abilities. In Mmapapo's case, all her children excelled academically and pursued careers in law, health sciences and teaching. In Mawe's case, all her children were gifted artists, singers and creative people. Mmapapo made a point that none of her daughters would be denied the right to access education. She stood tall as a beacon to remind her girls that they had everything it took to make something of themselves in the world.

My mother told me that the only time she and her siblings received anything new was when their father came home to visit over the December holidays. He was a handsome man, with a permanent broad smile. He was well built but short, with muscular arms marked by two tattoos on either side of his biceps. There was an anchor on one and a red rose on the other, signifying a tumultuous past and gentler winds in later life.

Together with her younger sister, Selekane, my mother was sent to live with and look after their ageing and ailing grandmother, Belina. As much as she recounted with visible pain the loneliness that came with being uprooted from her nuclear family, she spoke highly and fondly about being reared and nurtured by her blind and entrepreneurial grandmother. This is from whom she must have learned how to nurture and love: the kind of warm love that sustains you long after she has left your presence; the kind of love that forces you to be self-reliant, independent and yet vulnerable. Without being aware of it, she also infused in me the urgency and importance of having a sense of purpose and to show up for whatever that purpose is. She was always in a hurry, impatient, distracted and jittery. This was perhaps driven by her heightened sense that life was not forever. Her strides were short and fast. She did not take kindly to those who plodded leisurely and aimlessly through life.

As a young, strikingly beautiful woman who travelled to the City of Lights, my mother was steadfast in her knowledge that nursing was her calling. She had been influenced by her eldest sister Mmanku, who had made remarkable strides in the profession. Desperate to change the course of her life, my mother enrolled at the nursing school in the biggest hospital in the southern hemisphere, Baragwanath Hospital, in Soweto.

11

1283

It was 1988 and I was nine years old. Unlike walking from 511K to school, our new home was quite some distance from school. By modern standards and with better roads and ease of transportation, our new house was about 13 kilometres from Kwa-Phalo. At the time, however, given the lack of tarred roads and absent interconnecting modes of transport, travelling from Naledi to school felt like an eternity. The public transport system consisted of one unreliable and overcrowded train and having to take multiple taxis.

My father owned a baby-blue Toyota Cressida. We called it by the first three letters of its registration number. JCP. Although JCP looked pristine on the outside, every time my father inserted the key to start the ignition in the early hours of the winter mornings, my sister Naniwe and I would clasp our hands together, squeeze our buttocks and say a little prayer in the hope that JCP would roar into action and take us safely to school without getting stuck.

On one particular morning, we had woken up at dawn as usual, so that we could make it from Naledi to Meadowlands at no later than 7.45 am. Our neighbourhood was situated near a wetland, where winters were particularly brutal. JCP would park on what was aimed at being a covered garage, but it did not have a roof yet. My father had to start and warm the engine for at least ten to fifteen minutes before departure.

On this day, JCP started to overheat. Badly. Nani and I were horribly let down by our morning ritual, which was ineffective that day. My father's stress and perspiration had become obvious. His attempts at pouring water into the radiator came to naught. When he finally stood beside JCP, smoking his cigarette and with a helpless expression on his face, I knew that this would be the day I would receive the teacher's wrath.

There was no use looking at the time at this point. My father had an uncanny ability to communicate his emotions in absolute silence. Without saying a word, he abandoned mission JCP, grabbed our hands and we began to walk to the train station. His nerves, anxiety and disappointment were as thick as the mist in the reeds that led to the main road. We had no choice but to keep up with his much longer strides. Arriving at Naledi train station after walking for twenty-or-so minutes introduced another layer of trepidation. Everyone moved at lighting speed in fear of missing the next train. The number of people set on their individual paths resembled an army of ants.

As we arrived at the platform, our train was leaving. We had missed it. After half an hour or so, a maroon-and-grey train approached our platform, accompanied by a siren, and this sparked a glimmer of hope.

In anticipation of our entry into the train, Babam clasped our hands tighter and lifted us high above the door beside him before the train could come to a standstill. Babam managed to pull us both up before the doors closed. The scene inside the train sent my heart palpitations into overdrive. I remember not being able to breathe because of the sheer number of people. At some point, Babam's palms had become so moist that he had to work harder at keeping his firm grip on our hands.

On the train, a preacher with a Bible in his hands was spreading the Good News to the 'congregants', who were seemingly oblivious to the danger only I appeared to be feeling. Some commuters had managed to find a seat and were glued to their newspapers. Kids, who looked my age and younger, were selling fruit and vegetables, moving up and down the coach with surprising ease and unassisted by any adults. The train preacher enjoyed a fair amount of attention, but most of the commuters were not bothered. The ticket examiner with a cane in his hand walked up and down, inspecting whether commuters had paid their dues. He did so while looking like he would relish an opportunity to use the cane on an unsuspecting but deviant commuter. I was intrigued by how outnumbered he was and how pointless his job seemed, given the ungovernable nature of the scene.

I kept myself distracted from the horror of the experience by reading the names of each train station as the train stopped. Merafe. Inhlazane. Ikwezi. Dube. Phefeni. When the train stopped at a station, it felt like a wave of hundreds of people would enter. By the time the train arrived at Phefeni station, which was our stop, it was so woefully overcrowded that there was no space to manoeuvre to make our way to the exit door. I was soaking wet with sweat, and the tears were running down my face.

As I was squeezed in between the fiasco, my father lost his grip on my hand, and I caught a glimpse of him raising Nani onto his back and then onto his shoulders. I watched as he almost threw her out the window into the hands of someone who had managed to exit the train before us. In a matter of nanoseconds, it was my turn to be pulled and thrust into the hands of my father, who now had Nani beside him.

I wailed all the way from the Phefeni station to school, ashamed that my younger sister seemed entirely unaffected and oblivious to one of my worst childhood experiences. My father did not pass up the opportunity to remark to Nani how brave and strong she had been and what a crybaby I was. Leaving the train station was not the end of the road. We still walked another twenty minutes to Kwa-Phalo.

I envisioned two possible scenarios in my mind, as I did with every situation. One, which was the most ideal, was that of our father walking into the school, bright-eyed and with us beside him, sitting down with the teacher, the two men having a civil conversation about why it was that we were late, and that conversation ending in handshakes and smiles. The other scenario, which was the most likely but dreaded one, would be of us walking into the school premises, trembling, no questions asked and told to line up against the wall to receive the dreaded punishment.

On this terrible morning, I was the unlucky recipient of the teacher's infamous lashings with a snake-like whip, skilfully and purposefully cut out from an old tyre, which landed cruelly on the buttocks; and if you were a girl like me, with a school dress just above the knee, the excruciating lashings would land on my thin-skinned, pre-teen, bare thighs. He did not hold back, mustering his entire physical force and might, and certain to leave blood-stained scars on my fingers, which served as a line of defence to mitigate the power of the lashings on my thighs. He was intent on carrying out his mission, with his eyes opening widely, synchronised with the blowing up of his cheeks. Each lashing was more painful than the previous one, until the skin was numb.

He was tall and lanky, sported a balding Afro, and clad in bell bottoms and floral shirts in a dress sense quintessentially from the 1970s. These lashings gave him a visible sense of satisfaction. He invariably ended his sessions with a grin on his face.

The injustice of having been victim to the teacher's lashings lingered much longer than it should have. I found it particularly troubling that the world around me appeared oblivious to my pain. No one commiserated with my emotional and physical injuries. I soon realised that this was par for the course. I was extremely touched by the fact that my lateness was due to no fault of my own, yet I was on the receiving end of a physical attack from a grown man, who carried out his cruelty with no need to account to anyone. Although a quiet and introspective girl, I felt unduly silenced.

Trains signified places of trauma for me. Once or twice on the train, there were hordes of men with red bands on their heads and carrying machetes, spears and knives. These men would also descend from the nearby Dube Hostel in their hundreds, which often led to the school principal promptly dismissing school. Dube Hostel was a no-go area. Just walking past, I did not even want to look in its direction. You knew it was an ominous obscurity, a structure that stood as a reminder of schisms within township life, and a tense relationship between the 'outsiders' and the 'locals'. Living a stone's throw away from our house in Ipiva Street, the men from the hostel were known to most of us as members of Inkatha, which was made up of mostly Zulu-speaking male migrant workers who lived in male barracks-styled structures, socially and economically removed from nearby communities. They were not quite blended with the community. Life at the time was defined by the possibility that one could die from a stab wound or gunshot caused by 'amaZulu', as we referred to them, or the fear of being whipped at school or at home. I lived in constant fear long before I knew the word existed.

LEFT: My maternal great-grandparents Belina and Molefe Matseke. My maternal grandmother Mmapapo was a toddler when Molefe passed away in the 1920s, while working as a mineworker in Boksburg. The site of his grave is unknown.

BELOW LEFT: My maternal grandmother Elizabeth Mmapapo Mametse (right).

BELOW RIGHT: My maternal grandfather Rapereng Michael Mametse (right).

TOP: Mawe (Winnie Sesi Khemese) and Tata (Nkwenkwe Elliott Themba Khemese) in the backyard garden of 511K, with the children of the Band of Hope during a meeting.

ABOVE: My grandfather, Tata, conducting the Meadowlands Zone 3 Methodist Church Choir, which always won competitions. On the extreme left is Richard Muntu Masote (my great-uncle), and Mawe (my paternal grandmother Winnie Sesi Khemese), singing soprano, is third from left.

RIGHT: My paternal grandparents. Mawe and Tata's wedding day.

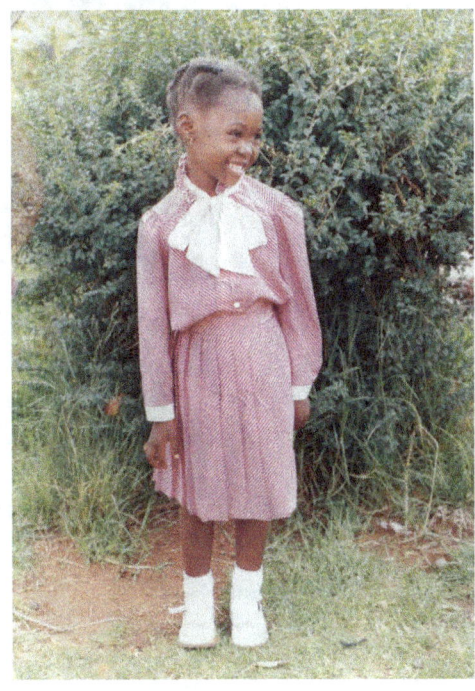

TOP LEFT: My mom, Tale, during nurses' training.

TOP: On Mawe's green couch at 511K, where I spent my early years.

ABOVE: In the backyard garden at 511K, during the days of the *Ikhaya Labantwana* television show.

LEFT: At 511K, with my dad, Babam, Naniwe and me (with the Afro).

The painting, signed 'Verna', which held my attention as a young girl.

At my paternal great-grandparents' (Sekolo and Johanna Masote's) home in Mzimhlophe, Soweto, with JCP, the family car. From left: My cousin Molefe Mametse, my sisters Naniwe, Ntombizone, Fuziswa and me.

From left: Ntombizone, Nomfundo as a baby, and Fuziswa at 1283.

Practising the violin at 1283.

Dad performing while shooting a music video.

From left: My uncle Sandile Khemese, Thamsanqa Khemese, my father, Makhosini Mnguni and Walter Sisulu, before the Soweto String Quartet professionalised as a full-time band.

Tombstone unveiling of my paternal great-grandparents, Johanna and Sekolo Masote. My aunt Nonceba Ndlhovu with her twin sons Xolani and Xolile Ndlhovu (my cousins), Tata, Mawe (in the hat), Ntate (Michael Mametse, my maternal grandfather) and my mother carrying my last-born sister Nomfundo.

My BA Law graduation at Wits (2000).

My LLB Wits graduation with Mawe, Mom and Dad (2002).

As a first-year candidate attorney in my office at Werksmans in Sandton (2002).

At my first home in Bryanston, with my dad, my mom (in pink) holding my daughter Ntsumi, Fuzi (next to my dad), our cousin Kabelo Monnathebe, me (right) and Nomfi in school uniform (front) (2007).

On my wedding day, 30 October 2010.

With Arthur, on our wedding day.

Our wedding day, with my in-laws and the Mabasa family. Back row: Caroline Mabasa (sister-in-law), Ezekiel Vilankulu. Middle row: Arthur's brother Douglas Mabasa, with sister-in-law Sylvia Mvundlela. Front row: Our son Urhandzile Mabasa, daughter Ntsumi Mabasa and nephew Amukelani Mabasa.

On holiday with the family in front of Chief Albert Luthuli's home in Groutville in KwaZulu-Natal, with Arthur, Akani and Ntsumi (in pink) in December 2011.

On holiday in Thailand, where I received a message from President Ramaphosa in August 2018.

My birthday celebration in 2016 with our family. From left: Urhandzile (Rhandzo), me, Akani sitting on me, Arthur with Rixaka sitting on him, and Ntsumi Mabasa.

At my 40th birthday celebrations, with Mpho (left) and Busi.

David Hertz, speaking at my 40th.

Neil Kirby, at my 40th.

Nomfundo's baby shower in November 2021, with Naniwe, Ntombizone, Nomfundo, Fuziswa and me. (© NANDIPHA KHEMESE)

12

Shades and Textures of the Land of My Birth

It all came crumbling down like a ton of bricks one summer's day while being driven in a school bus. My face was up against the window as we drove past a queue of jacaranda-lined streets in the northern suburbs of Johannesburg. I was a ten-year-old who was naturally keenly aware and attuned to the world around me. The air itself was different. It was crisp and fresh, combined with the scent of summer leaves and the whiff of jasmine. The soil was midnight black. It was not the red-tinged, dry kind that I had been accustomed to in Meadowlands. This was rich, fertile and moist. It was not the kind found in Soweto, where dust was blown in from the mine dumps, especially in the autumn. In winter, the coal-fired stoves found in every household would create a dark lining in the skyline.

Here, it was nothing like that. The streets were suspiciously pristine, appearing almost abandoned. They were notably tarred, with clearly marked zebra crossings and actual pavements. I hardly spotted any activity or even people walking in these streets – there was none of the eclectic energy of Meadowlands. It was sterile. There was not a shred of litter in sight. It was still. The kind of quiet that made you notice the sound of your own heartbeat. There were singing birds, which made me wonder why it was that I had never noticed the sound of birds in Meadowlands. There were splashes of water from garden fountains.

The silent, high walls made a statement. It was the kind of silence that made one instantly self-conscious. Despite my curiosity to know what lay behind the high walls, it was not difficult to conclude that the huge houses were a no-entry zone. They were certainly not meant for *us*. I caught a glimpse of the odd tennis court and swimming pool, and I secretly wished the bus would stop momentarily so that I could take it all in. The endless sprawl of manicured lawns suddenly made Tata's pride and joy – his patch of lawn in our backyard – look like a silly undertaking.

Here I was, in this bus, discovering a parallel existence I never knew was there – just 30-or-so minutes from the grounds of Kwa-Phalo Primary School. My ears became deaf to the racket of my peers and the war-cry singing that was taking place on the bus. My eyes were wide open, literally and figuratively.

I had not quite understood the fuss from our school principal the week before. There was a frenzy and panic after it was announced at assembly that our netball team would be competing against another school. This was to be a different kind of match, where we would be bused to the opponent school. This was a deviation from the norm because we always walked to the opposition, supported by a gang of non-players, whose role was to cheer us on along the route, set to intimidate the opponents with flair and song. This time, we were to play a netball match against a *white* school. But that was not the half of it.

Principal Mbele had urged us to ask our parents to buy a white pair of takkies, white shorts and a white T-shirt. This felt hurried and superficial. It was well understood that few parents would afford to fork out their hard-earned cash on a once-off netball game, so, like how most things worked, it was common for children to borrow or barter for school needs and resources. We had been accustomed to playing our matches on the grounds just outside the school yard – an open field. The rocky ground with weedy bushes was our netball court. It was difficult to imagine why we were suddenly expected to buy a special uniform, as we always competed with other schools from Soweto in home clothes of our choice.

As we arrived at the white school, it felt like I was being teleported into an alternative universe. The fact that I was wearing the pure white takkies that my parents had managed to purchase at the last minute paled into insignificance. The netball court was immaculately green and meticulously painted with white lines. Standing on that netball court, I felt smaller and smaller as it appeared bigger and bigger with each passing moment.

For the first time, I knew what it was like to feel diminished. Little did I realise that I would spend most of my life vacillating between the cycle of diminishment and fear and responding to it with copious amounts of sheer willpower to take me to the next phase of my struggle.

I was rudely interrupted from my fleeting but hard-hitting state of victimhood when I was approached by a white girl from the host school. Her skin was like porcelain, and she had blue eyes and wavy blonde hair that glistened under the sun. Her hair was tied up casually in a high ponytail, with a few strands that kept flying in and out of the sides of her mouth. Now and again, she flipped the sides of her hair, removing it from interfering with her clear view of me. This was not the type of mannerism I had ever seen before. I wondered what her hair tasted like in her mouth and why she seemingly did not find it strange or even disgusting. She and her team were clad in identical regalia: navy-blue skirts and matching tops, with the positions of each player printed on the back. Like me, she was the captain of her team. She played centre, while I played the goal attack position. She stretched her hand towards me to greet me, with my team behind me and hers behind her. She was perky, welcoming, *free* and unburdened. The kind of freedom and sense of place and ownership that I had not witnessed in a child my age. At least, not where I came from. They appeared genuinely happy to host us, and yet we were petrified.

The lines on the netball court were solid, and the umpire made a point that each team member was placed accurately in the correct position, behind the correct line. This was the first confusion. At Kwa-Phalo, our game was a lot more fluid, and our grounds were rough and ready. With our game, you instinctively knew where your position was and where the boundaries were, without having to rely on drawn lines to keep you in check.

I realised then that there was a code to the game that we were ignorant about. Every time we had the ball, which was rare in this game, the umpire would abruptly blow her whistle: '*Foot fault! Time! Obstruction!*' Our game was fast, aggressive and electric, with room for flair and creativity. Theirs was measured, steady, methodical and clinical. My team members and I were not familiar with any of this, nor could I respond adequately to the exasperation and defeat our team was experiencing. We were annihilated. The champions of Meadowlands had fallen flat on their faces. Our opponents were graceful, stretching out their arms to shake our hands at the end of the game.

Until this day, it had not occurred to me that the solid state of my being was in fact wanting or that I was somewhat blinded and short-changed. The smug warmth and love I had been showered with under the asbestos-laden, 100-square-metre roof at 511K suddenly tasted venomous and inadequate. All that I had clung to for dear life was exposed as something short of a lie.

I uncovered a bigger world that gave me a glimpse of the rest of rich, white, urban South Africa, and I would navigate it for some decades to come. I could not unsee this piece of discovery.

Beyond feeling and being battered, an insatiable seed was planted that day: what if *I* too wanted to be in this world? What if I could speak the English language with as much poise and polish, with words rolling off my tongue effortlessly? What if I could be like that blonde girl at the host school? The mere thought of this filled me with a strange exhilaration, embarrassment and shame. Another thought struck me: who had created this world? Why were there such tangible differences? Could this horrible situation be helped in any way? These thoughts and questions developed into an internal, silent mission and intrigue.

Most importantly, the Meadowlands netball champions had not lost because we lacked the talent and know-how. We lost because there were different rules of the game that applied. We lost because we failed before the game started. We knew we fell short. We lost because we were swallowed by the knowledge that we did not belong. We lost because the game we were playing was not the game we knew. The rules that we had not known were the rules that determined if we won or lost. These rules had no room for our world view, where we came from and our living conditions. These rules required us to alter ourselves, to discard all that we had known and held dear. These rules stripped us and erased us to a place of irrelevance.

I was met with a level of intrigue and an awakening once again between 1991 and 1993 when Babam enrolled me at Topaz Secondary School in Lenasia and my younger sisters, Fuzi and Zone, at the nearby Pentarosa Primary School – both Indian schools located in an Indian township. Although they were not Babam's first choice of schools, they suited his pocket.

Topaz afforded me the first glimpse of just how pervasive and intricate the racial composition of the country was. I became accustomed to the differences between Islam and Hinduism, those who spoke Urdu and those who spoke Gujarati. I came to know and experience the religious and cultural tensions that existed in both groups. It was the first time I was taught in English as a medium of instruction, a marked deviation from my Xhosa-centric primary school.

Although my command of English was more than acceptable, I found myself internalising the sheer state of difference around me, such that the content of the curriculum played second fiddle. The learning and observation that I took in was not in the curriculum, it was in learning and understanding the racial and political depth and breadth of the politics of my country.

I learned the difference between a burka and a hijab, as many children would come to school in their religious gear. I took an interest in my friend Shivani's mehndi and nose ring and the meaning behind them. Although an outsider in the main, I felt a distinct kinship in this school.

The social ills played themselves out, as they did in Meadowlands. Faizel and Razaad went from straight-A pupils to drug addicts in one term. Shehnaaz was impregnated by a schoolteacher. The drug trade had spiralled out of control in the townships, such that some areas in Lenasia were notoriously dangerous and marked by gang violence.

Although on some levels better than Kwa-Phalo, there was no clear, blue swimming pool, sprawling lawns or pristine tennis court. With little competitive sports, the focus was clearly on academics. Evidently, there was more to South Africa than just Meadowlands and the white school we had visited in the white suburb. Topaz introduced me to complexity and the layers between black and white. It was my glimpse of what lay behind the seemingly monochromatic state of the country.

I felt a familiar affinity with and warmth from the aunties on the street corner who sold us China fruit and *choria* after school. Although I sensed the religious and cultural distinction between Muslim and Hindu people, the sense of community was unmistakable.

Back at 1283, a burgeoning community was forged. The small neighbourhood of about 30 families became one harmonious village of blue- and white-collar workers who had big dreams for their children. Living in close proximity meant that my mother could go next door to the Mokoenas' house if she was short of sugar while baking.

The Dube family lived diagonally opposite our house. Bra Spot worked for himself, having earned a reputation of being the best mechanic to fix old BMWs. At any given point, his yard was brimming with the classic 'matchbox' 3 series, the 5 series and M classes. His daughter Khosi became a sister. Khosi, Nani and I formed a trio called 'Friends with Style'. We were heavily influenced by the dominant African American culture of female pop stars like SWV, Jade, TLC and Salt-N-Pepa, against whom we benchmarked ourselves. Beyond what felt like a repressive childhood, we lived in our heads and imagined our lives past the four corners of our home and the two lousy streets that made up our small and irrelevant neighbourhood.

The Mkhize family lived three houses away, with two daughters and two sons. Babu Mkhize was a policeman, and Mam Nokuzola was a teacher. Nani became best friends with Zandile, and I with Thembi. They were people just like us and hailed from the older townships that were similar to Meadowlands. This was the land of promise and great expectations.

Bra Peter lived next door to the Mkhizes' house. He was famous for blasting Motown classics from his radio, which was placed strategically at his front gate, at volumes that would compete with conversations we had in our home.

Ma Moroka's house was diagonally left from our house. She did not have children, she was serious and strict, and her home was spotlessly clean and pristine. God forbid if a ball accidentally entered her yard while the kids played on the street. No one wanted to experience her wrath. Her cold demeanour melted away during the school holidays when she would gather us around and laugh belly laughs that exposed her natural beauty. She found joy in turning our varied talents into song, dance and acting.

Rosemary Maake lived right opposite our house. She was strikingly beautiful and organised the annual Miss Naledi Ext 2 pageant, at which I was crowned queen in 1992. This was much to my father's amusement, because how was it possible that I beat Khosi, who, according to him, was more beautiful than me. Such was his humour.

Babam had a special friendship with Ntate Kgotleng, a man who loved and believed in all the children in the area, and who cared about our safety as much as he did about our education and general well-being. He was what stitched the community together as a place where we all felt we belonged. In us, he saw what the future could be – beyond the conditions that prevented him from catapulting to new heights. He was the local patrolman, counsellor, connector and motivator.

In a sense, 1283 soon found its shape, form and substance as part of a small community. I took a great interest in storytelling, writing plays and scripts, taking up leading acting roles and singing. This place held a mirror on who I was and could become.

It was at 1283 that I started to become attracted to boys, but, at the same time, I was terrified of the idea of dating. Every time I had a crush on a boy, I was reminded of the moment when Tale sat me down and closed the door behind her. Her message was clear: '*Now that you have started your period, it means you can fall pregnant. Stay away from boys. You play and sleep with boys, you fall pregnant.'* She left the room before I could ask all the questions that remained in my head. This conversation left me feeling immensely guilty for having crushes on boys.

The feeling was conquered after a secret love interest that no one knew about – except for Nani. She knew everything. I lived entirely in my imagination. It was safe. It meant I dwelled in an imaginary world where I could be free enough to actually date – and be safe.

In real life, I did not have the need or the chutzpah to venture into scary and controversial things like kissing or touching. Besides, Babam's sixth sense and attention to detail was so sharp that I felt he could see right through me, even as I was innocently washing the dishes and fantasising about a boy.

One time, a boy who liked me, and whom I liked back, gave Nani a Chanté Moore CD to give me as a Valentine's Day gift. Babam – a man of few words who was driven more by action – put me into the Cressida and asked me to direct him to the boy's house. Incensed that I even knew where the boy lived, we parked in front of his house, and the mission was clear. Return the CD. Case closed. I felt dirty. You could have sworn that I had committed the cardinal sin. It did not help that I was completely oblivious to the interest many boys had in me. My fear for Babam prevented me from even noticing.

December holidays were a time when Babam's antennae were particularly alert. I was once standing behind the high wall on the street, talking to a boy who thought I was attractive and smart. He looked at me with abounding vulnerability. I felt the same way too. Convinced that this was a safe moment as our faces grew closer and closer, out of nowhere The Hawk appeared. '*Nothing escapes me. I always see beyond.*' The man was right. It was pointless to try to deceive him in any way.

Tale and Babam had successfully managed to create their own identity in their own home, both as a couple and as parents, away from the abiding and mightiful 511K.

In between 511K and 1283, Marapyane was a regular feature nearly every December holiday. The contrasts were vast.

Marapyane was everything that 511K and 1283 were not. The drives felt far too long and boring. The barrenness and open tracts of land that separated Joburg from this rural area became interesting only when we noticed cows grazing in the fields. Most of the drive was on gravel road. As JCP struggled to drive through peaks and valleys, rocky terrain and red dust, I wondered how my mother got to Joburg in the first place. But once we arrived, everything stopped. The stillness of Marapyane outstripped the strife that it took to get there.

We were greeted by an imposing mulberry tree and a once yellow, now rusted borehole, where we manually pumped water from the ground. The pump elicited a screeching sound, rhythmically mimicking the pumping process. I could taste the metal and sometimes the sand residue in the water. Evenings were particularly dark outside, contrasted by a galaxy of the brightest stars. The crickets' rhythmic array of song pierced the silence of the night. Nature did not have to compete for its legitimacy. It loomed large. From my bare feet stepping securely into the warm sand, carefully dodging the rude thorns, to the rooster taking control and crowing at the crack of dawn, Marapyane explained who my mother was.

The roaming chickens and livestock in the kraal made me realise how self-sufficient the people were. I took joy in taking walks through narrow pathways on the sandy soil with my cousins to visit my uncle, Victor.

The simplicity and slow pace of Marapyane was an obvious contrast to Soweto. The walk to the long-drop was a particularly scary undertaking that was debated beforehand with Nani. Then we would walk amid the shrubs and vegetable patch, past the kraal and into the tin-demarcated structure. Like with everything else, nothing happens without Naniwe. Looking deep into the long-drop hole, while squeezing my nose tightly with one hand and balancing the other hand on the makeshift seat, resulted in me avoiding liquids and eating as little as possible. I wondered how it was that people here accepted that this was their reality and, more importantly, how they were seemingly comfortable with the status quo. The thought of my tiny body sitting at the wrong, miscalculated angle and falling into the pit often occurred to me. The visit to the toilet was always a risky undertaking that was eased only by Nani's reassuring and brave demeanour.

Tale had a different bounce in her step in Marapyane. She owned her every move. She was home and self-assured. She was the centre of attention and, by extension, so were we. Our maternal grandmother Mme opted to refer to each of us as '*bo ntombi*', which colloquially means 'the girls'. Being *banyana ba ko Jobeke* meant we felt judged and othered for many reasons: for failing to wake up before the first rooster crowed, for failing to make afternoon tea for the elders without being prompted to do so, and for failing to shine the grey concrete floors so that they resembled a mirror. A girl's currency was placed on how much physical labour she could muster. My sisters and I fared woefully. We simply did not measure up. Tale, by contrast, worked like a horse, sure to protect us from the unspoken yet significant scorecard. She did this by taking up the cleaning, cooking, ironing and everything else that was considered to require female energy.

Unlike at 511K or 1283, where there was a confluence of different spoken languages, in Marapyane everyone spoke seKgatla. Speaking isiZulu or isiXhosa was unheard of and caused laughter from our cousins.

Marapyane was to me a demonstration of how direct the relationship between land and its inhabitants was. Food came directly from the ground, the livestock were fed from the ground, and here there was no shortage of space, as each homestead had a dedicated area for animals, grazing and crops.

The land itself was vast compared to dense, dirty, bustling, busy and boisterous Soweto. Here, most people walked barefoot, almost a signifier of their grounding, not only of the body but of the mind and soul too. The lemon tree outside the kitchen was always the meeting spot for banter and necessary shade for the parked cars in the blinding heat. In a cathartic sense, time stood still in Marapyane. The land spoke for itself. It nourished. It was nourished in return.

PART 2

A New Dawn

13

Blooming

The year 1992 was a turning point in many ways. Babam had finally yielded to his life's purpose as an artist, composer, founder, performer and cellist. He left his nine-to-five job at South African Breweries at the ripe age of 39. Watching him grow into himself was magical. It was like witnessing the blooming of a flower right before my eyes. The courageous decision he took to formalise the Soweto String Quartet ushered in a new chapter for our family. He freed himself from the shackles that held him back. I watched him dedicate his heart and soul into building the Soweto String Quartet brand. The man had ascended to a higher level of himself.

My strict, domineering, overprotective, uptight and socially reclusive father became my sounding board and a muse overnight. He would walk around whistling a movement from one of his many collections of classical music.

The symbolism of 1992 signalled not only the rebirth of Reuben Malusi Khemese, but it also coincided with the beginning of my life as a teenager. More importantly, it was the coming of age of a mutual, deep love, affection and connection between father and daughter. I was suddenly not spoken to but spoken with. My opinions were actively sought out. To my father, I mattered.

The Soweto String Quartet struck gold almost instantly. It was awarded a contract to be the resident entertainment band permanently based at the newly built, five-star luxury Palace of the Lost City at the Sun City Resort, owned by the hotel magnate Sol Kerzner.

My father, the cellist, founder and administrator, together with his younger brothers, Sandile (lead violin) and Thamsanqa (second violin), and their childhood friend Makhosini Mnguni – the boys from Meadowlands – had the first real opportunity to turn their love of music into an expression of themselves and to earn a decent living.

South Africa was slowly emerging as part of the global community after the ravages of apartheid. The political trajectory of the country was clearly changing. While the eyes of the world community were on South Africa, my father and uncle's dreams were being realised on the world stage. The Khemese brothers and Makhosini Mnguni represented the hopes of the country when they were chosen as the musical outfit to perform at the Miss World pageant to be hosted by South Africa.

The blooming that was taking place was foreshadowed by bloodshed and darkness. Earlier in 1992, the political violence and tension between the ANC and a group affiliated to the Inkatha Freedom Party (IFP) led to the bloody Boipatong massacre. There was no way to hide, unsee or ignore the ravages caused by this tragic event, which claimed 45 lives. Seeing multitude bodies covered in foil and blankets became commonplace. It was the subject of conversation whichever way I looked – in my own home, in telephone conversations and in newspapers. Brenda Fassie's 'Boipatong' immortalised the emotion of this time in her song featuring Tshepo Tshola.

To my young mind, this was a time of great confusion. Looking at the elders' sunken eyes and helpless banter, I did not know whether our country would sink into civil war and what civil war would mean. Civil war was a term that was bandied about frequently. I had no doubt in my mind that this period was significant. It mattered which way things were going to be after Boipatong. It felt like the entire nation was walking a tightrope.

This was not only a story one saw and heard in the news. It led to the sudden loss of friends to areas unknown. My father's cousin, Attie Lehlongoane, was involved in student politics at the University of the North (then known as Turfloop) and a member of AZAPO. One day, he unexpectedly moved into our house at 1283. We were told as children never to mention him being there. I remember him being snuck into our home in the depth of the night. I eavesdropped on late-night conversations that he and Babam held. I did not quite understand my uncle's involvement and connection to the massacre. What I knew was that there were underground forces that were planted to respond to the IFP's resurgence, and this involved even more spillage of blood.

Just three years later, everything turned around for us. The Soweto String Quartet was becoming an international phenomenon. Nelson Mandela was ushered in as the first democratically elected president of South Africa, and he chose this band to travel and perform with him in various parts of the world. The distinguishing features and metaphorical value of the Soweto String

Quartet were firmly rooted in the group's heritage and identity. The musicians breathed their life experiences of struggle and dispossession into their instruments, resulting in a unique brand of Afro-jazz compositions, some of which were known struggle songs. It made sense symbolically why Mandela would pick the group as his fellow disciples to spread the message of reconciliation. The album *Zebra Crossing* and their zebra-striped ensembles represented the hope for a reconciled and diverse country.

The glowing success of the Soweto String Quartet also signalled the next chapter of our lives as a family. Babam had previously told us as kids that one day we would have a home where we each had our own bedrooms, a swimming pool and a study. He said it so many times that it appeared he spoke this dream into existence.

Babam's musical preferences were also undergoing a drastic change. He was suddenly vibing to Boyz II Men, Paul Simon, Sting, Gladys Knight, Eric Clapton, Brenda Fassie and Ladysmith Black Mambazo, and he had acquired a certain bounce in his step. He found himself as a composer and creator of his own original works. He sought our opinions, and we were both affirming and ruthless when we needed to be. Our family unit was entrenched, enchanting and free.

One day late in 1995, Babam took Nani on a drive. He did not say where they were going. He thrived on pleasant surprises. They drove up the hills and curvy turns of the southern suburbs of Johannesburg. As Nani recalls the story, she marvelled at the stunning homes nestled neatly between one koppie or the next, lush with greenery and with large tracts of land. They arrived at a home that was still occupied by an Afrikaans-speaking couple and their two small children. They were welcomed by the woman, walked in and Babam proceeded to ask Nani: '*So which one would you like to be your room?*' Not only did Mandela become the president of South Africa of a democratically elected country, but our father had also fulfilled his promise to us of a home where we each had our own bedrooms, a swimming pool, a study and a lush garden. This was the chapter of dreams fulfilled in our lives.

This newfound freedom was met with a sense of pride in our new home. It had imposing palm trees, rose gardens, a driveway, antique furniture, art on the walls and a refrigerator that matched Babam's exquisite palate.

Babam instantly became a world traveller, bringing home to us every bit of experience, artefact, musing and literature he was gaining in the world. All his senses were awakened. His ideas and views of the world became increasingly progressive and ultimately liberal. He would go on tour for months on end to virtually every part of the world, but he always returned to pour into us all that knowledge and learning. We were a safe, loved and privileged family overnight.

Babam and Tale spent hours on end chuckling, debating and loving each other in our new home. Their friendship re-emerged. The Khemese sisters – Bulelwa, Naniwe, Fuziswa and Ntombizone – were their pride and joy. Although our bond came naturally, it was fuelled and nurtured by our parents. Our new home fitted us like a glove, with winters spent sprawled like lizards on the underfloor heated tiles and Babam's signature vegetable-and-bone soup cooking all day long.

Babam's awakening was not only his. It was also Tale's. She had been championing a campaign in the public health system to promote the breastfeeding of infants. While Babam found expression in his work as a performing artist, composer, networker and head of the quartet, she found her voice in her field as a midwife, which led her to take on an Honours degree in nursing while still in full-time practice. She was a midwife by day and a student by night, while being a mother to four daughters and practically holding the fort when Babam's career reached its peak.

By the time Tale graduated with her Honours degree, our youngest sister Nomfundo was born in November 1995. She was the baby that was born into glory and success, when my mother was entering her forties. I still remember when Babam arrived back home with a gleeful smile on his face, exclaiming: '*It is yet another girl!*' I will never forget visiting my mother at the hospital after she gave birth to Nomfundo and gleaning from her tired face that it had taken a toll on her tiny body.

This was the year that the Soweto String Quartet was awarded three significant South African Music Awards, following the release of their world-acclaimed debut album. This period also saw my mother settle and prosper profoundly in her role as a mother and nurturer in our home. By all accounts, observing how they poured themselves into their own crafts and development, they injected a sense of purpose and drive into us children. This taught us how one shows up for life.

14

The Greys within the Rainbow

Not only were we now living in leafy and pristine suburbia, Nani and I were enrolled in a new school in the northern suburbs of Johannesburg – Waverley Girls' High School in Highlands North. Intrigued by seeing long-bearded men in black hats and jackets walking in packs and sometimes with their young children did not at first register to us as an indicator of a neighbourhood that was occupied predominantly by Jewish people.

I had not even heard of the existence of the religion or the community until then, nor did I question or associate the fact that school ended early at 11.30 am on Fridays as a signifier of a particular religious inclination or a community that was different from where I came from. I had observed that some teachers clearly wore wigs, without realising that was in fact a religious practice for orthodox Jewish women.

It was increasingly evident that the election of the first black president was not suddenly going to eradicate apartheid in its form or substance. Our parents' financial upward trajectory and their ability to afford a better-resourced school were not enough for us to be enrolled at a school of choice without a hassle. Apartheid's spatial planning remained as racist as it was the day before Mandela was inaugurated as president. White people still largely lived in the white suburbs, with sprinkles of a few black families that had somehow escaped the shackles of a racist regime. The reconciliation project was not seeping into white establishments fast enough, if at all, and schools were not spared. Most private and state white schools still maintained policies that required learners to reside in close proximity to the school. What this meant was that it was difficult, if not impossible, for a child who lived in the black townships to access education in schools that were located in the white suburbs.

Babam, ever so resourceful (and stubborn), managed to get us enrolled at Waverley by using the residential address of one of the Soweto String Quartet's Jewish managers who lived in Highlands North.

The lack of a residential address in Highlands North and surrounds was not the last of our woes. It was just the beginning. It was an uncanny introduction to systematic and systemic years of subconscious othering, exclusion and subliminal racism that was meted out to black girls at the school. It was not overt, but it was pervasive and effective. It played on our individual and collective psyche and self-conceptualisation.

Black girls were overwhelmingly in the minority at the school. Common utterances from some teachers included: '*Don't speak that language here.*' '*This is not Soweto.*' '*Why are you girls so loud?*' '*This is not a taxi rank.*' We knew that our presence at the school was merely tolerated. I could not shake the feeling that I did not belong. A small gathering of a group of black girls somehow signalled danger, and an effort was always made to 'separate' us.

The curriculum did not speak of African excellence and brilliance, let alone the languages and their place within the African continent. I could not find my ancestors in narratives about glory and triumph. I could not locate Mawe and Tata's uprooting from Sophiatown in history lessons, nor was Tata's history as a mineworker digging for gold even a topic. My history lessons spoke nothing about the violent and bloody ways in which my ancestors defended the land of their birth. I did not learn of the contribution of African people in the advancement of mathematics. Achebe, Serote and Wa Thiong'o were absent from English literature.

Learning about Louis XVI, Bismarck and Napoleon felt so far-fetched and ultimately erased the little sense of self that I had left. Each time I listened and learned about the various wars and battles of white men of yesteryear, I wondered whether these white men's appetites for power and domination over others were somewhat of an inherent trait that came with whiteness. Each time I came across a depiction or impression of their faces in textbooks, my mind drifted and wondered if they looked in any way like Malan and Verwoerd – both names that were vilified as enemies of black people.

In my teenage mind, there was everything fundamentally wrong with my mother tongue, my complexion, the size of my nose, the hair on my scalp and, indeed, where I come from. I wanted so desperately to be seen and to matter, and the only way I figured I could achieve this was as clear as the light of day: I needed to un-black myself. Thoroughly so. I needed to clothe myself in whiteness; learn it and mimic it until I reached acceptable levels of palatability. I was undone. The years of standing firmly fortified by my grandparents and parents were whitewashed, simply because that was the price to be paid to access decent education and some semblance of a peace of mind.

My accent subconsciously became progressively anglicised into a suburban twang as I paid extra attention to my teachers' and friends' accents, intonation and how and where the tongue rolled and twisted. My natural, short hair felt crusty to me, leading me to relax my hair. I found myself softening my voice and altering my mannerisms to appear more delicate. There was a need to distance myself from the imposing boldness, loudness and sometimes even the hardness that was associated with blackness. Soon enough, no thought was paid to how easily the words rolled off my tongue.

The change in the law regarding the admission of black children to white schools and the installation of the new government did not offer protection against the feelings of unworthiness that black girls brought from their poorer homes. They did not shield us from the fact that we had to be up at least three hours before our white counterparts, just to be able to access better education that came with resources and sporting codes we had never heard of before. We arrived home at sunset, having taken two taxis and a bus twice in the day. Most of the other black girls were also caregivers to their grandparents and younger siblings. Housework was not a chore but a responsibility and a way of life.

The danger of the reconciliation project was that it was a further denial of the structural existence of apartheid in every sphere of life. It lacked an important aspect – that of reparations and social justice. It required of black people not only to awaken themselves from the trauma of an inhumane system but also a denial of a moment to pause and reflect. The euphoria of the 'Rainbow Nation' overshadowed the need for meaningful and substantive change and an intentional effort to understand who we were and how it was that we came to be where we were. There was no room to process our trauma, let alone possess the language for it. The black townships remained as black occupation camps, and public transport remained overcrowded, under-resourced and unreliable in the form of taxis, trains and buses. The mine dumps remained prominent on the outskirts of the townships as reminders and fortresses of the apartheid system.

In the classroom, there was no recognition, let alone allowances, made for the fundamental, visible and palpable disparities that existed between black and white girls. For me, an assumption was made that because I came from an inferior and less-resourced school, I had to repeat Grade 10. I turned fourteen in October and had already passed Grade 10. However, the school policy was that I was far too young for Grade 11 and that I needed to repeat Grade 10 and take all my subjects on the lower grade.

I took this setback as a personal challenge. I put my head down. I had to work harder than most. I got home most days at 6 pm; in the winter months, this was well after sunset. Given that my mother was a nurse and midwife at the peak of her career, housework largely fell on my shoulders. By the time I was ready to focus on my schoolwork, it was usually well after 10 pm. I survived on four hours of sleep. Despite this, I was completely ignorant of my unique circumstances, nor did I view my life as a plight. It was simply a case of the cards that I was dealt. There was never a time that I felt that I was short-changed. I simply needed to step up, and I did.

By the time the second term came, I had worked so hard that I had done well enough to take my subjects on the higher grade. I quietly executed a plan not to be faceless and voiceless. This was my first lesson about existing in a predominantly Calvinist, white and Western-dominated world – I had to work significantly harder than my white counterparts, having significantly less. Less resources. No sense of belonging. I spoke less and observed more. I noticed when a teacher was far more engaging with particular girls in the class and not others. I noticed when a teacher was morbidly dismissive or even vaguely disinterested. I also noticed that when I spoke up in a history or English class, the teacher would gaze at me a little longer – expressing surprise at my depth and command of the language and considered opinion.

The might and reach of the underlying apartheid legacy did not swallow the human kindness and the grace that was bestowed on me by most of the teachers in the school. I deliberately stayed out of trouble and was always mindful of the cost of the fees. Most of what drove me to seek excellence was the palpability of my parents' past struggles.

My deep feelings of self-doubt were revoked in history classes where my opinions were sought after, on the netball field where I co-captained the team, and in English classes where I had a natural flair and affinity for literature and poetry.

As the teachers poured themselves into me, my self-consciousness withered away, bit by bit. In Dalene Matthee's *Kringe in 'n Bos*, I explored and felt a kind of humanity that was not clothed in the blanket of apartheid. In Alan Paton's *Cry, the Beloved Country*, I discovered that the racial schism in South Africa was mainly rooted in land dispossession and colonialism. It was curious to me that we were taught that the history of South Africa was said to have commenced in 1652 and that Africa was referred to as the 'Dark Continent'.

Mine was an existence drenched in complexity and nuance. On the one hand, I devoured Shakespeare's *Macbeth*, and I buried myself in 'Sonnet 116' at breaktime, feeding into my imaginary world of romance. On the other hand, I was intrigued by S.E.K. Mqhayi's *Ityala Lamawele*, which I borrowed from Tata's expansive Xhosa literature collection.

Although there was no explicit agenda for the teachers at Waverley to immerse us in principles of feminism, there was a fierce bias and effort to that effect, particularly from the headmistress, who embodied what in my view was the picture of a strong, accomplished, intellectually astute and liberated woman. Nothing about what she inculcated in the girls gave us any inkling that we were in any way defective, weak or 'less than'. Her brand of discipline appealed to the self to find a unique place in the world. It was the kind of discipline that was empowering, enabling and a breath of fresh air.

The day had come. Weeks prior, the topic of conversation at the library, at the tuck shop, in the quad, in the corridors and on the sports grounds was who would be chosen as prefects in our matric year. I had not, for one second, anticipated making the list, although

I was secretly hoping I would.

When the usual ceremonial aspects of assembly were done, the headmistress stood in her characteristically upright stance at the podium. *'Now, girls, we have finally reached the part of the programme where I will announce the new prefects for 1996, in no particular order. I will call out the first five names, please come up to the front as you hear your name being called.'*

Bulelwa Khemese was the first name that was called, sounding utterly unreal, and much to the delight of my fellow pupils. I rose.

Our paths had collided. The white, blonde girl I had met when I was ten years old at that netball match in Parktown became a peer, a fellow prefect and a fellow leader. I was seen. I meant something. I mattered. This was the kind of validation that I had not only sought externally, but it also served as a revelation to me that there may in fact be something of deep value in who I was and who I could become.

15

Freedom

It was a significant year. I was reintroduced to myself. I took longer to look in the mirror, when previously I had only managed to catch a fleeting glimpse before hurriedly looking away. But things were different now. I noticed details in my face I had never cared to pay attention to. I appreciated the texture of my hair and the bright smile on my face. My neck was elongated and slim. I was beginning to like the person who looked back in the mirror. Could I be pretty? Dark-skinned *and* pretty? As much as it sounded like an oxymoron, a little voice in me dared to imagine that it could actually be true.

I was turning seventeen and I was deeply consumed by the raging fire that burned inside me. If anything, my final year at high school served as an igniter and a catalyst that awakened the spark in me.

In the preceding years, I could not keep my eyes away from the television screens that were dominated by the Kempton Park negotiations, led by Cyril Ramaphosa and Roelf Meyer. The two men represented the ANC and the National Party respectively, and the negotiations would lead up to the promulgation of the Constitution. The air was thick with the promise of the birth of a new and emancipated country. The converse was also a possibility. Even at that age, I could sense the tension and fear that it could all come crumbling down and degenerate into chaos and bloodshed.

It mattered to me that both Mandela and Ramaphosa were trained lawyers. I watched and listened closely when they spoke on television. I was drawn to how they spoke, the words they chose and how they carried themselves. To my mind – and not to suggest the exclusion of many other men and women who were at the forefront of these negotiations and the struggle itself – I wondered how their legal training may have been invaluable to the mammoth task of negotiating and ultimately delivering an arguably peaceful transition towards a free South Africa. In a way, this solidified my interest in pursuing a career in law.

The end of my matric year coincided with the promulgation of the Constitution in 1996. Like my country, I was rewriting who I was to become, hoping to create an identity that would be built on the sum of my experiences and the past. The new Constitution signalled a renewed purpose and a road map towards reclamation, restoration and renewal.

A new possibility existed for the restoration of land and social justice for the dark-skinned girl in the portrait at 511K.

16

Enlightenment

I prepared myself in every imaginable way. How I would walk and talk. I had no doubt about which courses I would enroll for as part of my degree – law and psychology.

This was my reintroduction to the world. As just me – not the first-born responsible child and not the well-behaved school prefect. The mask was off. I was fearless but not careless. I was ready to grab the next five years of my life with both hands.

Tale had given me several lectures about how I needed to survive and thrive at university, which I took in earnest. She had, after all, recently spent a year at the former Rand Afrikaans University (now the University of Johannesburg) completing her Honours degree weeks after the birth of Nomfundo. She attended evening lectures when she was not discharging her full-time midwifery duties. I had overheard her motivating, counselling and sharing her university study material with other women her age, cautioning them not to give up. I had also heard her telling an exhausted colleague about how valuable she was, and how the kids would grow despite the balancing act of being professionals, students, mothers and wives.

She was the ringleader — a cheerleader even. Her peers followed her lead because she had sufficient conviction, driven by hope and a larger societal purpose.

She passed on to me how she poured herself fully into her roles. By the time I entered my first year at university, she had armed me with pearls that proved priceless. She explained to me that attending classes was entirely voluntary and that no one would be chasing after me. She told me about the importance of maintaining and sustaining a relationship with my lecturers and tutors. I learned from her that studying had to involve exploring and researching material beyond the prescribed reading.

As empowering and affirming as she was, she also let it be known that Wits University would spit me out instantly if I did not have my wits about me or walked in there with an inflated sense of superiority. Key among everything that I took in was the importance of preserving and keeping my humanity. She insisted that the lecturer needed to know me by name as much as the cleaner in my residence and the clerk in the fees office. In fact, *I* needed to know *their* names. Her interest in the next human being was not measured by that person's ranking in the perceived social and economic stakes. She alerted me to the fact that there would be students from abroad, the townships, Model C schools and private schools. My mother taught me to make it my business to get to know and spend time with all of them.

South Africa's unequal society was glaring on campus. This ranged from children of kings and queens in Africa, children of the nouveau riche, children of immigrants and those who had to put together a few cents just to have a meal at the end of the day.

ENLIGHTENMENT

My room-mate at Jubilee Hall was a woman twelve years my senior. She was studying teaching and hailed from rural Limpopo. Her grasp of English was poor, but her sense of purpose and determination was something I did not readily see in students from affluent homes. She had to escape poverty, and this was why she was at Wits. Nothing in between mattered.

'Mphako, make sure Bulelwa doesn't get swallowed by the system, thinking she has arrived and is cool. Call me when she starts missing lectures.' My mother loved the fact that my new room-mate at our residence was so much older than me, grounded and from a rural background. She may have seen herself in Mphako.

As much as I knew that it would please my mother if I approached my new life at university the way Mphako did, I was still just almost eighteen. This was my newfound freedom, and I certainly was not about to spend it all at the Wartenweiler Library.

I arrived on campus right in the middle of orientation week when the besties and new friendships had either formed in high school or were made earlier that week. The campus was massive, divided into the East and West Campus. University was a leveller. In that first year, I recognised the past pupils from Topaz Secondary. I even bumped into Pretty Munyai, my academic class rival from Kwa-Phalo, who was enrolled for a BSc degree.

Naturally, I gravitated towards a group of twelve girls who had come from all-girl, Model C and private schools. The narrative was similar: black middle-class parents who worked way harder than they should have, sacrificing to ensure that their children escaped the insatiable claws of poverty. These were the girls who told stories of being shocked at seeing their mothers' salaries as nurses and wondering how they even managed to put food on the table. We were the generation of 'first blacks', and we were in the minority at the first multiracial schools – the girls who needed to disassociate from blackness to thrive.

We were those children who did not know what it felt like to have a mother or father regularly attend hockey or netball games, because our parents could not afford to have a second away from making a living. Some of us were called up on assembly stages to receive various awards without knowing the applause from and seeing the pride in the faces of our parents. It was drummed into our heads that we dared not ruffle feathers. We were to devour the curriculum fed to us, because that was an antidote to a life bedevilled by strife.

We were the generation that had to grin and bear being 'othered', because we were promised a pass on the other side. We were thought to be the 'better blacks'. For a while, we too believed that we were indeed better, until the cracks began to show.

Back in our grandmothers' homes or the 'family home', we were constantly taunted for 'acting white' and reminded about how defective we were as Africans. Our kinship was woven together by displacement and a false sense of privilege. To stand out, black girls in these environments had to demonstrate superhuman abilities and an extraordinary type of excellence. It was never going to bode well for a black girl to coast through.

Before you knew it, the 'better blacks' congregated at the upstairs canteen on East Campus, where lasagne and other hot meals were sold for no less than R100 a plate. This was the allure of privilege that my mother had warned me against. I saw in action exactly the world that my mother did not want me to inhabit blindly, devoid

ENLIGHTENMENT

of any social awareness. I dwelled uncomfortably in it, knowing internally that my reason for being there was much bigger than being in the 'right' crowd or the twang in my accent. The kids from Model C and private schools even had code names for our counterparts from Limpopo and the Eastern Cape – the SRBs. Strong Rural Background.

The excitement of finally moving out of home lingered in the air for days on end. I devoured the opportunity to be anonymous, to recreate myself as I went. Wits found me ready and prepared, and I was woefully captivated.

In the lecture theatres, the sheer number of students struck me. This was in stark contrast to the 25-pupil classroom. The other new experience was the unfettered freedom. The freedom to pick where to sit. The freedom to be punctual, late or not to show up at all. The freedom to wear lipstick to class. The freedom to sleep in.

I knew inherently that I would be interested and captivated, but I had not anticipated how insatiably drawn I would be to every syllable uttered by Sakhela Buhlungu in sociology class when he first introduced the concepts of agency versus social structure. He was unassuming and soft-spoken, but you could sense the oasis of his knowledge. It mattered to me that he was a black man lecturing in a traditionally white institution of higher learning that was held up by its colonial past. I felt that the knowledge that he was imparting was not simply theoretical but was textured by his own life experience as a Xhosa man with roots in the rural Eastern Cape.

Soon into the first year, the socio-economic divides manifested in the student politics of the day. When the nouveau riche class of black students was filling up the student parking lots, students who hailed from the townships and the rural areas were bemoaning bread-and-butter issues, fighting against academic and financial exclusion. Although I inherently believed in the righteousness of the cause and the struggle, I admittedly felt fundamentally unaffected in that my father was effortlessly footing the bill for my fees. Politics could not be separated from Wits, and Wits did not separate itself from politics. The student movement was vibrant. The Jewish students were involved in the South African Union of Jewish Students, the South African Students Congress was vociferous in pursuing a pro-poor agenda, and a new formation of leftist students known as the International Socialist Alternative was pursuing a multiracial student formation. I could not locate myself among these movements, and yet I could not quite fully articulate why none of them spoke to me.

My Model C education placed me in a position of privilege in that English was my first academic language. I was able to adapt and grasp the academic material with ease. My counterparts from township and rural schools had to sometimes take on an extra year of study designed to bridge the gap that had been caused by the unequal education system. Many of these students had never learned in English as a medium of instruction.

At this point in 1997, the university residences were almost 100 per cent filled with black students. Most white students were day students.

I have never drifted from the intention to become a lawyer. The mental visual of me standing in the courtroom before a judge and fighting the battles of the black girl in the portrait had played in my mind like a movie since that conversation with my father.

ENLIGHTENMENT

Beyond the lecture room, Wits University unleashed a world where the silenced generation of black children dared to find their voices. This was the year in which YFM, a popular, black youth-run radio station, was launched. It was the first time the 'Mandela-freed generation' asserted its voice, struggles and triumphs on a public platform – owning its status as the youth that was breastfed and soaked in apartheid but graduated in white-dominated schools and the black townships alike.

Kwaito groups and artists such as TKZee, M'du, Trompies, Mashamplani, Boom Shaka and Thebe owned the social scene. The concerts on campus were electric. It was evident that something important was unravelling in front of our eyes – victimhood to triumph. We were becoming, rebelling, reforming and recreating. We were embracing our blackness, unapologetically. This period saw the formation of township- and kwaito-inspired clothing brands by Loxion Kulca. Television was filled with images of Wits students as presenters of Channel O or other music programmes. Thandiswa Mazwai, the lead singer of Bongo Maffin, was my immediate next-door neighbour at Jubilee Hall. Nhlanhla Nciza, the lead singer of Mafikizolo, then shy and quiet, was regularly seen at our residence. There was also a substratum of a former Model C and private school class that was united beyond race. Danny K, a Jewish artist who was involved in the music business, typified this new era. He was often seen hanging out with the coolest crowd of black students at the concourse, before dashing out in his grey Opel Kadett. These people were not stars or celebrities at the time – they were young people in an academic space, forming their identity and place in the new South Africa.

A NEW DAWN

What was being subconsciously embedded was the idea that the stage was ours. Our time had finally come. Being the children of Mandela, we truly believed we could have it all.

The internet was not even a word in our vocabulary. In the lecture rooms, the buzz word was 'globalisation'. We were learning about the impending new world order, where borders and boundaries would no longer have any real impact.

Dwelling in the world of all these possibilities, I came up with the idea of a campus-based radio station that could link up and connect with other campus radio stations abroad to share student experiences and bridge the gap that had been formed by the division of the world into its various categories: the north and south or the first and third world.

When Babam told me he would be hosting the one and only Quincy Jones in Soweto's famous Wandi's Place, my mind ran away with me. As Babam routinely demonstrated to me, according to him, I was always good enough to be in the room or around the table in the midst of statespeople, superstars and influential personalities. Dinner with Quincy Jones was one such occasion when my father was not going to leave me behind. He did not feel the need to prepare me on how to be or what to say. He simply needed me to show up and be myself. We arrived early at Wandi's and were welcomed by Wandi himself. Babam had often taken us as a family for Sunday lunches at Wandi's, so he was no stranger to us.

Soon enough, in walked Quincy Jones with two of his colleagues. He was a friendly, boisterous, larger-than-life character – both in stature and in the energy he radiated. At an opportune moment, Babam struck up a conversation that led me to explain my concept of a transcontinental campus radio station. Quincy was both attentive and engaged. He listened to my ramble and immediately handed me the business card of his colleague, who was then the head of Q Radio. It turned out that Quincy was already dabbling in radio.

What else was possible?

17

The Law

My first law lecture was a monumental let-down. The study of Roman law had no immediate sense of relevance to me. It was based on pre-existing notions, rules and values, with strong roots in colonialism. It was racist, patriarchal and paternalistic.

A legal view must be based on and justified by a source of law – either an existing statute or a court decision. To be fair, this was not only a feature of the study of law, but it was also much the same with the study of sociology, international relations and psychology. Knowledge and academia were grounded on authority, prior knowledge and sources.

Unlike at school, where knowledge was based on the regurgitation of what was largely in the textbook, at university, knowledge was tested and evaluated on one's ability to critically analyse information and ground one's thinking and opinion on existing theory. One had to delve into the theories of historical writers and their different approaches before one could venture an opinion – whether this was Grotius, Freud, Pavlov, Durkheim, Marx, Weber or Du Bois. Academia was a humble reminder of how little one knows.

THE LAW

The Constitution was brand new, having come into effect in February 1997, literally in the week I started university. Most of the material still referred to the Interim Constitution of 1993. A few months earlier, South Africa was a society governed by a parliamentary sovereignty. The promise and hope for an egalitarian society were yet to unfold. Inside and outside the lecture room, history was changing right in front of my eyes. The new Constitution was hailed globally as being one of the best in the world, and it was to drive substantive change and justice in South African society.

I am not quite sure what I had expected in the first year of studying law, but I had anticipated that there would at least be a legal case about Steve Biko and the apartheid regime's complicity and guilt in his persecution. Or maybe there would be a case study about how Tsietsi Mashinini's family could access justice for his mysterious disappearance. It most certainly was not so.

There was an air of elitism in the lecture room in how law was taught and in the use of language. Something about it was exclusive, inaccessible and foreign. The terminology was riddled with Latin words and phrases. The lecture room was fraught with an air of inequality. You saw it, felt it and could almost touch it. The students from traditional apartheid schools tended to be quiet observers, unlike the vociferous and confident participants from white schools. Some dared to challenge the lecturer and probe his or her ideas. This level of conviction and ownership of the space was something to behold. Each lecture room was like a snapshot of South Africa – from those who could afford to buy all their textbooks to the ones who had to line up at the Law Library to use the two or three copies of each textbook. It was the difference between those who hopped into their cars to travel back home, those of us whose parents could afford to pay for residence, and the sea of students who hurried out onto Jorissen Street to take taxis to the Bree Street taxi rank and then on to the outskirts of the townships.

When the first semester results came out for my law modules, I stared at the noticeboard at the Oliver Schreiner Law School, barely believing how badly I had done. I had failed all three of my modules.

I had not grasped that this was not the study of waffling. The study of law was not about freestyling. I had to understand and apply the principles and read and absorb long and often user-unfriendly court judgments. The study of law was an institution itself and was institutionalised. It was predetermined, and there was no scope for instinctive radical thought.

By the end of the first year, I had firmly grasped the formula of studying and thriving in my law subjects: from reading case law attentively to remembering the case citations and extracting the most relevant principles contained in the leading cases. More importantly, the set formula entailed the ability to eliminate irrelevant facts, to determine the body of law being examined and ultimately to apply the hypothetical facts to the legal principles. Constitutional law as a course grabbed me without it even trying.

By the second semester, more than half the number of students who had opted for law had crossed the floor to more interesting and palatable courses. Many choose to study law for the noble purpose of changing whatever they perceive to be perverse and unjust about the world. Some choose to study law because family members told them that they are so talkative that they would do well in law.

THE LAW

Studying law, however, unwittingly channels all that energy into a non-negotiable mould that may not, in the long run, inspire changing laws or society but rather inculcate a generation of lawyers who are likely to maintain the status quo and drive pre-existing and pre-ordained laws and principles. It is therefore of little wonder why law classes became smaller and smaller as each semester passed.

In my final year of my postgraduate LLB, as part of the constitutional law elective, we had the freedom to choose any subject of interest for our dissertation. It was not difficult for me to end up with a topic that compared Section 25 of the South African Constitution with the Article in Zimbabwe's Lancaster House Agreement. To me, land dispossession was by far the most pertinent and effective by-product of colonialism. If I was to make my five years of study count, it was going to be focused on one of the most important constitutional rights contained in the Bill of Rights: the land reform agenda.

The arduous hours spent researching and writing my dissertation were the formative mental and psychological genesis of a seventeen-year journey that led to the call from the president in August 2018.

At the end of my degree, I was left with more questions than answers. In my courses, I could not locate the trajectory of the land laws and wars that had culminated in the Natives Land Act. I did not come across legislation that existed pre-1913 that enabled the forced removals and systematic dispossession of indigenous Africans as part of the curriculum. What was visibly missing from the studies was a deliberate focus on how unequal land ownership and land redistribution in South Africa was institutionalised by the law itself. Nor did I find ideas on how laws and policies could be improved or developed to achieve meaningful land redistribution.

My thirst and hunger to know more about the subject was far from quenched.

18

A Glimpse into Practice

'*I want you to listen in on this telephonic discussion.*' I duly complied. Babam made a call to his attorney: '*Hi, Derek, how are you? My daughter is studying law at Wits, and she's looking to get a sense of how law firms work. She wants to become an attorney. When can she come and see how it is in the real world?*'

I was given the opportunity to do vacation work in a medium-sized but by no means insignificant firm at Rabin Van den Berg & Pelkowitz. Derek Rabin was highly regarded in entertainment and commercial law, and he represented the Soweto String Quartet in their recording deals. I had eavesdropped on numerous conversations between Babam and Derek. On occasion, Babam insisted I read through the many drafts of the recording and publishing agreements. It made no sense to me that the recording artists were entitled to no more than 2 per cent of the sales of the album. I understood the commercial aspects of the capital outlay that went towards recording, distribution and marketing, but it still felt to me that something gravely unfair was at play. I had, for the first time, come to realise the exploitative nature of the creative arts industry.

Who determined this 'global standard', and why was it considered acceptable and just?

It was at Rabin Van den Berg & Pelkowitz that I first held a real-life client file, in yellow folders with thin blue stripes. The lawyers were all incredibly busy, and I soon figured out you were lucky if you were greeted or if a lawyer actually looked up from the document their eyes were glued to. The associates were already at the office before I arrived. When I left after sunset, it was clear they were nowhere close to leaving the office.

My eyes were opened to commercial and corporate law. This was the advent of black-owned conglomerates. I learned of commercial structures and deals that bore the names of Safika Holdings, Mawenzi Capital, Mzi Khumalo and Saki Macozoma. The Black Economic Empowerment (BEE) policy championed by former president Thabo Mbeki had taken root. I experienced first-hand how Mbeki's neoliberal policies culminated in the nature of instructions that were being done in law firms. A new class of black multimillionaires and even billionaires was being formed.

The complicated structures were clothed in trusts and special-purpose vehicles. I found it interesting that there was no obvious capital outlay or equity laid out by the BEE partners, which meant that funding instruments were invariably by way of debt financing. It was also intriguing to me that in many cases the beneficiaries of BEE were former freedom fighters who had strong links to the ANC and the Tripartite Alliance. It occurred to me then that even within the scheme of new-found freedom, the economic benefits were not to filter through to Mawe and Tata, nor to the extraordinary people of Meadowlands.

A GLIMPSE INTO PRACTICE

The most important lesson I took from my first experience at a law firm was the disconnection between studying law and the skills required in practice, most of which called for 'thinking out the box' and immersing oneself in practicality and the demands of the world today. No law course could have prepared me for understanding different ways to value a company or the vulnerability and courage I had to possess for the simple task of knocking on the closed door of a busy and overworked attorney to ask for 'some work'. This seemingly benign act prepared me never to take personally whatever response and treatment I got back. It was terrifying as much as it was humbling.

I walked away with the knowledge that there might be a place for me in the pursuit of justice in the commercial world, although the pieces had not quite come together yet.

The letter of recommendation written by the attorney who exposed me to various transactions and explained concepts I had never heard of affirmed me. My law studies were not in vain after all.

PART 3

On the Way to Becoming

19

A (Legal) Home

'*Werksmans, you say? I worked there in the fifties! In those days the firm's offices were in the centre of town. The other big firm was Bowman Gilfillan.*' It was one of those many visits Mawe and Mkhulu Muntu had around the oak table at 511K over tea and scones. Mawe's brother Muntu's eyes shone with pride when he shared this piece of history with me. I had not been aware that my great-uncle was connected to a firm at which I was about to spend my legal career. I firmly believe I was led and even sent by my ancestors to Werksmans.

My mind drifted as I pictured Babam's uncle in the 1950s, as a messenger on a bike or scooter or filing court documents, not knowing that more than half a century later his great-niece would return to Werksmans, this time as one of the lawyers and potentially even a partner.

In my final year at university, conversations morphed from '*Did you submit your assignment?*' to '*Have you applied for articles?*' and '*Which firm have you applied at?*' The air was thick with anticipation.

Five large law firms dominated the South African scene. I applied to all the Big Five, and I was called for interviews at three of them. My academic record was decent but not outstanding, with my marks being in the top 10 and 20 per cent for each course. I had studied enough to understand the course work, but I certainly did not pass up on having a full life on campus.

In my final year, there were obvious stand-out candidates who were the crème de la crème, not only by virtue of the quality and articulation of their arguments but also because they displayed a certain inherent confidence and conviction in their abilities.

My first interview was in an intimidating boardroom, with a 360-degree view and floor-to-ceiling windows. It was attended by four white, middle-aged men and a white woman who was head of human resources at the firm.

The atmosphere was cold and unwelcoming. I felt my barely 50-kilogram weight disappear into the black, fancy leather chair. I suspected they wanted me out of the room faster than I did. I remember one or two of them actually making eye contact. It was as if there was an unspoken code that made them all look as stiff as their ties choking their necks.

To my horror, one of the interview questions I was asked was whether I had intentions to have children and when that would be. Nothing could have prepared me for a question like that, and I was clearly taken aback. In the last five years, all I had thought about and invested in was becoming a lawyer. Having a family was not even a factor in my plans.

I realised that this question meant that I was sitting in a room of people who were not looking at a prospective lawyer. Rather, they were interviewing a *woman*. This made me extremely

A (LEGAL) HOME

uncomfortable, and I had to wonder whether a man would be asked the same question. But perhaps more flabbergasting to me was that places and institutions run and controlled by those who are supposedly the custodians of just principles, equality and human dignity are not devoid of prejudice and bias. Walking out of that room, I felt unseen, belittled and alienated. I most certainly was not going to pine over not making it into their articles programme.

The second interview I attended was with two male partners from another Big-Five firm. It was so apparent that I was part of a tick-box exercise. The interviewers were disengaged, and my time with them was far from memorable.

My search for a legal home continued.

20

9/11

It was 11 September 2001, and I woke up to absolute mayhem. The TV was ablaze with images of the bombing of the Twin Towers. All local and international news networks focused only on this surreal and traumatic event that gripped the entire globe.

But the significance of 9/11 had a personal meaning and attachment. This was the day I received a call that changed the course of my life. It was from human resources at Werksmans. *'I'm pleased to inform you that your interviews with our firm have been successful. Do you accept a position to be one of our candidate attorneys for 2002?'* This was precisely the firm I felt I would fit in with. I was elated. I could not stop the words from coming out of my mouth, but the human resources person had other calls to make to other candidates. I was polite enough to let her go. I wished I had, in that moment, verbalised to her just how meaningful this phone call was. I accepted.

I felt an affinity with Werksmans. First, Babam had indicated to me that Derek Rabin was previously an attorney at Werksmans before he left to open his own law firm to focus on corporate law and entertainment law. Second, my interview at Werksmans was the only one that did not elicit any feelings of unworthiness. It felt authentic, and the interviewer made an effort to get into my mind and heart.

The interview itself took place in the year 2000. It was on one of those beautiful early afternoons in the Johannesburg spring, with the scent of jasmine in the air. It is not an exaggeration to say I felt a sense of belonging the moment I was called from the reception area by one of the partners who walked with me to the boardroom. Our interaction was light but real, informal yet meaningful. The interview felt like an engaged conversation.

I was on the cusp of two worlds. My time as a student was coming to an end when I received a call from Babam, who was already parked outside. I knew something bad had happened. As I approached him, I noticed that Tale was also in the car. A giant had fallen. Our Tata had perished. I felt I still had so much to give him, to give back to him. This was a man who spoke my life into existence. He made it known to anyone with ears and prophesised that I would be a great lawyer one day. '*Uzokuba ligqwetha lethu.*' There was only one way to honour him.

21

Signed Up

I was as ready as I could be for my first day as a candidate attorney. Babam insisted that he would drive me to and from work every day. This was also my baby sister Nomfundo's first day in Grade 1. In her turquoise-and-white striped school dress, with her front tooth missing, Nomfi had the world ahead of her.

We jumped into Babam's embarrassing and over-the-top zebra-striped BMW, both of us feeling grown for different reasons in different seasons of our lives. Our sixteen-year difference as sisters did not matter at all. By all accounts, it was a significant day.

I chose to sit with Nomfi in the back seat. All was going well. *'Remember to smile, my baby, and don't forget to have the best time! Spot a friendly face and glue yourself to that person.'*

When we arrived at her brand-new school, it was clear we were not going to navigate through traffic in time for the beginning of my induction programme. And when it became apparent to me that Babam had no intention of walking Nomfi into her new school to ease her into the day, I knew I had to take matters into my own hands.

SIGNED UP

The outside gate was full of commotion – little ones with teary faces, some squeaking with excitement and others oblivious to their start of a twelve-year journey. I did not have time on my side, but this was one moment I needed to know that she was going to be okay.

Together we walked with the maze of parents along multiple corridors, searching for the hall where the new cohorts should be. The scene invoked the same emotions and reactions I had experienced in my school days. The feeling of being lost and swallowed.

I clasped her tiny hand tightly as a symbol of reassurance. I was intent that hers was going to be a different journey to mine.

When we eventually got to the friendly but visibly overwhelmed grade controller, she greeted us with a wide smile and scrolled down to find her name.

'*Oh, Nomfundo Khemese. She's in Miss Henning's class just around the corner. You can drop her off there and her teacher will meet her. Don't worry, she'll be just fine.*'

Momentarily unwilling to let go of her, I looked around and spotted another little girl who was as terrified as she was. '*Hi, little one. What is your name? This is Nomfundo. You can play with each other today and have lots of fun.*' I waved her goodbye with a lump in my throat.

By the time we had arrived at the company's new building in posh Sandton, I cringed as Babam parked right in front of the facade. The zebra-striped BMW screamed: '*Look at me, look at me!*' It attracted the kind of attention I loathed.

I was hoping to make a quick and unnoticeable exit from the dreaded monstrosity into the building. But Babam switched off the engine and walked into the reception with me in his signature peacock-style, slow walk, hands in his pocket with his pants high up above his stomach. I wished I could disappear into the nearest hole. He made a point of greeting everyone before I signalled to him that I really did not need him to hang around a second longer.

'*You're late. The rest of the candidate attorneys are in the seminar room. You've missed the first 30 minutes of the induction programme,*' said the receptionist in a part-contained and part-judgemental tone.

I trembled at the thought of walking straight into a long-standing stereotype – the new black girl, who was fashionably late, making a grand entrance.

As I quietly opened the door to the seminar room, the head of human resources paused mid-sentence and glanced up to see who was entering the room. The other eleven candidates all turned around to look at me. As I sank coyly into my seat with my heart pounding like a herd of elephants, I knew I had to calm myself down. This was the least favourable first impression to make among a group of twelve candidate attorneys who were going to compete for permanent posts at the end of the two-year period. I had made my first limiting career move, but I was intent on redeeming my tardiness.

Mawe's encouraging voice, Tale's words of wisdom, Mme's praise-singing at my graduation, Tata's look of pride, and Ntate's illuminating smile – all kept me fully aware of the magnitude of what was assigned to me. I took in earnest the seat I occupied as one of the selected candidate attorneys out of hundreds, if not thousands, of applications received two years prior. I had a deep knowledge that the opportunity I was given as a candidate attorney was much more than about the individual. It was a way to honour my lineage and my history, and a practical means to change the trajectory of where I came from.

The following two weeks were a blur and a whirlwind of information overload: all-day lectures about the IT systems, acceptable dress codes for the corporate world (especially for women), where to find legal precedents, where to find the High Court rules, softer issues around attitudes to non-legal, professional matters, and how to uplift, issue, serve and file court processes. I had never held a summons in my hands, let alone seen an actual trust deed or a discovery affidavit. I was entering a new world.

22

Tea Girl

The most important fortune or misfortune in the life of a candidate attorney is which partner you are assigned to for your articles. The legal secretaries revelled in the unofficial but important role of letting us know which partners were perceived as being affable and which were considered aloof. In the eyes of candidate attorneys, partners of the firm were distinguished not by how accomplished they were as lawyers or how much rainmaking they did. Their only meaningful currency to budding lawyers was their ability and willingness to be accessible, and to teach and impart legal skills, second only to their demigod status.

Reputations preceded names. Some were notorious for never keeping candidate attorneys for retention after the two years, while others insisted on being called 'Mr'. Several were known to be the better teachers, and some were plainly feared. We were made aware of the 'cancel culture' for candidate attorneys who made early but costly mistakes.

'*You are so lucky, you have been allocated to Mervyn Simon. He's the nicest principal of the whole lot.*' I had to wonder if the only black girl, and one of two black candidate attorneys, was perceived to have needed extra care and looking after and had to be allocated to the most nurturing of the principals of the firm. Granted, this was my own baggage that I was bringing with me. I owned it. It was there. But I could not offload it.

I found it very uncomfortable to refer to Mervyn by his first name. Having been raised in a home with strict notions of *ubuntu*, I was not going to dishonour the essence of my upbringing by disrespecting a man who was old enough to be my grandfather. No such discomfort was made visible by my peers and certainly not by his personal assistant. This was just one example of realising that my culture could sometimes stand antithetically to the corporate culture and vice versa. This meant that there was a level of suppressing my discomfort and personal world views and learning to assimilate a way of being. Assimilation is in and of itself disempowering. It was disempowering in a sense that it required of me to lull the fullness of my being: to lull Bulelwa from Meadowlands and to rather expose Bulelwa from Waverley. Having observed the formal corporate environment, I deduced that it was the anglicised version of me that would be palatable in my new environment.

Mervyn effortlessly made me feel at ease. After a few occasions of closing my eyes and calling him by his name, his name landed. He was an outlier of sorts. I quickly got used to his quick-witted and mischievous humour. Mervyn probed and quizzed my knowledge of High Court rules as much as he did my general knowledge about the world around me. It helped that we shared a love for dark chocolate and were both failed violinists.

Thanks to Babam, Mervyn and I conversed with ease about

Mendelssohn and Bach on our way to client consultations.

One day, he sent me upstairs to enquire about the status of a case he had been working on with another senior partner. Before entering the other partner's office, I approached his personal assistant, who had her head down as she typed away. Before I could tell her the reason for my visit, she kept her head down and muttered: '*No tea for me today, thanks.*'

Days later, I replayed the scene in my head. Here I was, so pleased that I had made it to the firm of my choice, only to be reminded that I was black and a woman, and those two descriptions could not have meant I was a budding lawyer in the building. There were no black female lawyers walking the corridors, so it was not a harsh assumption for her to have made at the time. It was reality. I had come to a strong mental resolve. I was going to capitalise on being unseen, put my head down and learn as much as I possibly could, so that I could prove to myself that I had all the makings of a respectable and respected lawyer.

This personal assistant had unwittingly delivered me a gift. She was totally unaware of it. I needed to take back my power.

In the end, to take offence at being mistaken for a 'tea lady' was somehow to shame, disrespect and even alienate the very women who had raised me, made me, anchored me and cheered me on. The tea lady *was* my grandmother, as were those who wished me well and prayed for me. It was that simple.

23

Belonging

Belonging is not necessarily about the big things. The cases. The content. The work. The rules. The formalities. It is about the soft intangibles. The jokes I could not relate to. The stories about pets I did not identify with. With insignificant banter came the realisation that we inhabited vastly different worlds. I was born into politics. I was a product of politics. It was counter-intuitive and interesting to me that my white counterparts found political discussions uncomfortable and misplaced at the lunch table.

A new incoming lawyer is handed the baton by the previous year's candidate attorney who was trained under the same principal. In my case, I had the fortune of walking into the shoes of Skhumbuzo Maphumulo. He was about four or five years my senior. Scrawny, intelligent and diligent. He knew all the corners of Mervyn's practice. He knew which document was filed where. And there were hundreds of files that spilled over to the end of the corridor and into the 'discovery room'. I had to endear myself to Skhumbuzo if I stood any chance of one day being able to see the wood for the trees.

ON THE WAY TO BECOMING

It was Skhumbuzo who taught me to be meticulous and care about the paper trail, how to file documents properly, the fact that pleadings are filed separately from notices, and that correspondence is filed with the latest on top.

One morning, when I arrived at 8.30 am, as was stipulated in my contract, Skhumbuzo called me aside. His face was stern, and his veins protruding through his temples were a sure sign that he was not impressed with me. '*Lalela, sisi, if you want to make it here, you arrive before Mervyn arrives. Mervyn arrives every morning at 6.45. The least you can do is get here at 7.00. This is not a job where you clock in at 9 and leave at 5. Here, no one owes you anything. You have to be ahead of your peers. First thing you do every morning is ensure that the filing of documents is up to date, and this is what you do in the evening before you leave. It is your business to read up on all those files, so that you understand what is going on. To do this, you will never leave at 5 pm.*'

I got it. I thoroughly grasped what he was communicating to me. Although embarrassed, I was grateful.

I only had Skhumbuzo to show me the ropes for two weeks, and I knew I had to suck as much knowledge and wisdom as possible from him. Soon enough, we struck up a friendship, and I had a trusted ally to help me navigate the Werksmans world.

Skhumbuzo had passed through countless hoops before becoming part of the Werksmans family. He had a daughter he was supporting in rural KwaZulu-Natal. He was unflinching and single-minded about ensuring that he build a home for her and that he gave her the best education. His work ethic inspired me. His drive motivated me. I wondered whether, in the fullness of who he was, his story, his battles and triumphs would matter at the end of his articles when decisions were made about retention. I found his lived experience rich and textured.

It was my first formal consultation with counsel. As we had been briefed during induction week, it was always the duty of the lowest-ranking junior in the room to serve tea. In this instance, that was me. Skhumbuzo nevertheless stood up to serve the tea as soon as it arrived in the boardroom. He did this so effortlessly that I stopped placing any form of value on it from that day on.

My love for exquisite clothing grew as my pay cheque grew. I quickly earned the reputation of always being dressed up and glamorous. I did not intend for it to be so. Dressing up every morning came naturally and effortlessly to me.

The Lady Glamour label made me slightly uncomfortable. I felt that it detracted from the essence of why I was there in the first place. To be seen and known as bright, hard-working, dedicated and committed would have mattered far more to me. It occurred to me then that perceptions prevailed more than reality ever could.

It took me a long time to discover that a sense of belonging is not something that is gifted to you in a beautifully wrapped box. It only happens when you have finally accepted who you are. It is the shift that occurs once you make the intrinsic realisation that you are the product of the tears, hopes and dreams of the men and women who have prayed for your upward trajectory, knowingly and unknowingly. Belonging is something you claim. It is there for the taking.

24

An Ambivalent Litigator

It was 2004, and I was retained as one of the eight candidate attorneys who would qualify as junior associates and later be admitted to the High Court.

My sights were set on becoming a top corporate commercial lawyer, not because that is what set me on fire but because that was the dominant narrative at the time. I did not get my preferred choice of area of law. That year, more demand was placed on the firm's dispute resolution department.

I was disappointed. All indications were that if you were to become a self-respecting and financially successful lawyer, banking and finance were the places to be. Mergers and acquisitions were the future of South African law. The country was open for business. A year prior, I had drafted myriad shareholders' agreements, sale of share and sale of business agreements, company and shareholders' resolutions, opinions about diectors' fiduciary duties, the King Code II and even exchange control matters relating to some wealthy clients. I was fortunate to have been allocated to partners Chris Moraitis and Tippy Luttig during my second year of articles.

AN AMBIVALENT LITIGATOR

Within that space, I was looked after exceptionally well by a senior associate in that team, Diane Bouwmeester. She was the proverbial dynamite that came in a small package. She was magnanimous about finding every opportunity to build my skills.

On one occasion, I had the opportunity to be on the sidelines of the Rand Commission, headed by Judge Johann Kriegler. I attended a session that was run by the then deputy governor of the Reserve Bank, Gill Marcus. To say I was star-struck is an understatement. I was impressed with how she commanded the room. In the spaces I had occupied until then, rooms were dominated by men. She defied what to me had been the script given to women.

When the chairperson of the firm called me into his corner office late that afternoon, my hands were trembling and I was prepared for anything. I had an inkling that I had done enough over the two years to stand a fair chance of being retained.

'I have the pleasure of informing you that you have been successfully retained as an associate of the firm as of March 2004. Welcome to the Werksmans family. I wish you a fruitful career.' I was elated.

My ambivalence about being retained in the dispute resolution department of the firm was rather short-lived. It soon dissipated the moment I was placed with a young partner who was in the throes of building a name in a practice area that was neither common nor sexy.

Neil Kirby was 29 years old, incredibly intelligent, sharp-witted, impeccably dressed and highly organised. Our forced union was not difficult to cement. There was a certain edge and familiarity that I could not put my finger on. It was one of those relationships where our minds met instantly without over-explanation. Neil's chosen practice area was timely. South Africa was gripped by an HIV/AIDS crisis that saw in the region of over three million deaths and approximately 40 million people living with HIV/AIDS in the country. The racial inequality caused by apartheid that persisted post-1994 placed a heavy burden on the public healthcare system, while private healthcare was comparatively more effective in delivering services to its largely white customer base. The tide was turning politically, as the ANC-led government was introducing health reform legislation and new policies that were aimed at reversing past injustices.

Neil's healthcare law practice gripped my curiosity and interest in a way that probably should not have surprised me. After all, being Tale's daughter, I had witnessed her undertaking community work at Tladi Clinic in Soweto, where she monitored the postpartum progress of mothers and newborns. She lamented the impact of poverty in the townships, which had a direct bearing on the well-being and health of her beloved patients. I reflected on Tale's passionate campaign in the 1990s that encouraged new mothers to breastfeed their infants for as long as possible. She initiated and led the Fatherhood Clinic, a campaign that encouraged men to be intimately involved as primary caregivers to both a new mother and a newborn. I discovered that 'healthcare' referred only to the formal system of heathcare as it exists within the pharmaceutical realm. My interest was piqued even further by the fact that the overwhelming majority of South Africans typically consult with *iinyanga* or *izangoma* as their first port of call and only access formal healthcare as a last resort.

It bothered me that even the laws and policies geared towards reform excluded the ordinary black South African woman on the street. Efforts at the amendments and introduction of the Medical Schemes Act, the National Health Act, the Pharmacy Act, and the Medicines and Related Substances Act all worked well if you were a member of a medical scheme with access to private healthcare services. However, these monumental and revolutionary laws and polices had no effect whatsoever on the poor majority.

Being raised by Mawe, I was curious to know whether it was possible to one day have *umhlonyane* form part of the Essential Medicines List, given its widespread use to treat ailments such as asthma, flu and other respiratory ailments. *Impepho* is used as incense not only as a gateway to communicate with ancestors but also as a method of relaxation and a stress reliever.

In healthcare, my love for law that matters was sustained. It felt like I was part of a whole that was moving the country somewhere. In assisting workplaces such as mines and organisations to formulate their HIV/AIDS policies, my immediate work involved one of the most topical issues in our national discourse. It meant I was reading up on the new policy documents and developing case law.

The ground was moving beneath us as clients sought Neil out to interpret the impending legislative changes, ranging from new legislation dealing with medical devices to the introduction of prescribed minimum benefits and designated service providers. I observed how Neil navigated building a name in this practice, and how it meant that he had to be at the centre of legislative developments.

The intellectual relationship we built soon spilled over to one that Neil had enjoyed years prior with Advocate Bruce Leech SC.

ON THE WAY TO BECOMING

Bruce had lectured Neil at Wits University at least a decade before I was a student. They both provided me with a fresh outlook. We became a threesome of friends and colleagues who litigated in various courts across the country. I appreciated the robust debates and exchange of ideas I witnessed between Neil and Bruce. In a room with them, I witnessed a soft waltz that sometimes progressed to a fast pasodoble.

Not every matter had to involve an advocate, and this is where I knew I would thrive: when a client walks in with a seemingly intractable matter, and where a fruitful resolution takes place without incurring the legal fees and the time-consuming nature of litigation. I understood that we were in the business of resolving complex matters for clients, and I grasped that some solutions may never see the light of day in the courtroom and others could only be resolved by way of litigation.

With Bruce and Neil, I was not only afforded a seat at the table, I also had the latitude to choose my own seat. They saw me, heard me and anchored me.

'*You seem to have double-booked yourself. We have a consultation at 10.30 on Tuesday, but that is when you are due to speak at the World Aids Day conference.*' Neil responded with his eyes fixed on the documents being stapled: '*No, I am not double-booked. You are speaking at the conference.*' At first, I let out a silly laugh, expecting him to tell me he was joking. The man was dead serious.

'*Your prior preparation determines your confidence when speaking. You will be the most knowledgeable person in the room, and this must be your comfort. Look slightly above the heads of your audience, and do not read your slides – refer to them.*'

AN AMBIVALENT LITIGATOR

As I was walking out of his office, he called me back in. '*You know I wouldn't do this if I didn't believe you have it in you.*'

I would not have known how ready I actually was had he not literally pushed me into the deep end. My belief in myself as a capable lawyer was honed and cultivated in this practice.

25

A Grandmother's Prayer

A vivid memory it will always be. Mawe was clad in her Sunday best: a knee-length, loose-fitting black frock and matching tulle hat were elegantly finished off with a set of pearls. '*I wish ukba u Tata ebekhona.*' Tale and Babam followed closely behind us as we entered the lift to the top floor of the newly renovated Palace of Justice on Church Square in Pretoria. The building greeted us with its imposing beauty, the marble tiles ornate and the pillars impossible to ignore.

It had been three years since Tata had passed on. This moment was as much his as it was Tale, Babam and Mawe's. It was the day of my admission to the High Court as an attorney.

'*Bulelwa Sesi Khemese.*' I jumped up as my name was called, and I nervously observed the judge carefully paging through my application and the annexures. '*The application is hereby granted,*' he announced as he tapped his gavel on his desk. All the hours that went into preparing, drafting and finalising the admission application were determined in that split second. I did not quite grasp the weight of the moment, until Mawe ululated as we exited the courtroom, and Tale and Babam embraced me with their teary eyes. To me, admission only marked the genesis of my journey; it by no means signalled an arrival. It was more of a formal crossing into the profession. I was far from where I wanted to be, but the moment was firmly and unquestionably theirs.

Mawe could always sense what my mouth could not utter, and she could see exactly what my eyes reflected. My career was undoubtedly on an upward trajectory, but she knew that it would never be enough to complete me. I was not aware that I lacked anything else beyond my budding career, my family and my circle of loyal friends.

Matters of the heart had not taken centre stage at any point in my life. This is not to say that I had not had my heart broken or broken the heart of others. I simply had not had a relationship that set my soul on fire.

While my weekdays were entirely taken up by work, my weekends consisted of late nights partying and clubbing with friends and acquaintances. These nights invariably ended in a rather predictable way. Nani and I would drive home in the wee hours of the morning, plotting and scheming how to enter the house without waking everyone. We bickered about whose turn it was to get out the car and walk across the lawn to knock on Fuzi and Zone's window, begging to be let in.

Fuzi and Zone, much like Nani and I, were like custard and jelly, peanut butter and jam. Inseparable. They were also smart and resourceful. Our late-night escapades and inevitable pleas to be rescued without upsetting the parents turned into their small but lucrative business. Fuzi or Zone would open the window ever so slightly. A thin arm would stretch out with an open palm and a R100 note would land, resulting in the alarm system being disarmed. The front door would be opened and Nani and I would be let in.

My debt-free, fast-growing income unleashed a newfound freedom for Nani and me. We were now living the life we had only fantasised about while washing dishes at 1283. We became the girls we had envied, dancing carefree in nightclubs and sipping on cocktails. We were invincible, and we were decidedly blasé to Tale and Babam's calls and pleas for us to slow down.

Underneath Mawe's unquestionable pride about my growth at work, she saw a layer of discontent underneath all the fluff. She was right. Mawe took one look at me when she came to visit on a particular day. It may even have been a visit that was orchestrated by Tale. Mawe knew exactly when it was time for her to unleash the big guns.

'*Guqa ngamadolo mntanam sithandaze*,' Mawe ordered. We both knelt down in the centre of my room. She stretched her familiar and wrinkly hands towards me and held mine. We bowed our heads before she proceeded: '*Thixo Bawo wethu osezulwini, ndithandazela lomzukulu wam. Ndithandazela ukuba umzisele umyeni ovela kuwe. Makube nguwe Bawo othi nangu kengoku umyeni, u Tata wabatwana bakhe.*'

I do not recall any other moment (and there had been many) when Mawe directed a prayer not to curb world hunger and not to pray for the sick or the downtrodden. This prayer was directed at me, with me. In that room there were three of us. Mawe, me and God. She intervened in the only way she knew. In that moment,

A GRANDMOTHER'S PRAYER

Mawe pleaded with God to send me my life partner, my fellow traveller and my true north.

26

Arthur

It was one of those balmy afternoons, but my mood could not even recognise it as such in my hangover from another failed relationship. My jadedness in the love department could easily have been misconstrued as an air of arrogance. I walked tall with a purpose. Sporting a below-the-shoulder black weave with a middle parting, dressed in tight-fitting black slacks and a black top and kitten heels, I secretly enjoyed being told I was too skinny.

I jumped into my car, put my seatbelt on and glanced into the rear-view mirror. I noticed a silver-grey Mercedes-Benz parked behind me, impeding me from reversing. Irritated by the idiotic move, I kept looking in my rear-view mirror, expecting the inconsiderate fellow to move his car. The man got out of his car, signalled to catch my attention and asked me to roll down my window. Reluctantly, I did so. My keen eye for fashion noticed the cheeky Abercrombie & Fitch bucket hat that was perched on his head in the most carefree way. I was immediately struck by his deep-toned voice that reminded me of Barry White. His approach was a mixture of casual charm and swagger, with an air of chivalry.

ARTHUR

He spoke to me in a KwaZulu-Natal accent: '*Wamuhle nkosazana ... ngicela inombolo ka Ma wakho. Ngifuna ukwazi phela ukuthi asho inani lenkomo eziyofuneka ze lobolo.*' My heart palpitated with each syllable he uttered. I elicited the most unexpected belly laugh when he told me it was my mother's number he wanted, not mine, so he could plan for my *lobola*. He told me I was beautiful, and he was sure he had met his wife.

I agreed to let him have my number when he jokingly threatened to refuse to move his car until I complied. In that short encounter, I experienced a variety of emotions: he irritated me, enthralled me, made me laugh, made me blush, and he left a lasting impression. That day at a parking lot at The Glen Shopping Centre, my heart met its match. Unbeknown to me, Mawe's prayer was answered.

PART 4

Heritage Meets Profession

27

A Mother is Born

It was a smooth and eventless pregnancy. Arthur and I had been in a fulfulling and fun relationship for just over two years. I was upbeat, active and beaming. My internal joy at carrying my unborn baby carried through to my physical being.

We were soaked and locked in a serendipitous physical, emotional, intellectual and spiritual connection that was oblivious to outside murmurs, opinions and disapproval. We were far from being considered the obvious picture-perfect couple in the eyes of the urban, black glitzy social scene. He was not a twanging guy who went to a Saint-something school. He was more of a beautiful mystery. He was already a father to a four-year-old boy, Urhandzile (Rhandzo for short). On top of my list of 'Nevers' was that I would never date a man with children or who had been married before.

Arthur was seven years older than me. He was Bantu school-educated and spent most of his high-school years escaping the sting of apartheid forces that were unleashed on students in Soweto and Alexandra. Unlike me, he was a student activist at the coalface of the struggle. His uncle thought it prudent to send him away from tumultuous and violent Chiawelo in Soweto in the mid-1980s to Tzaneen to focus his brilliant mind on his education.

It worked. Refusing to be swallowed by his circumstances and with two university degrees behind him and over a decade working as an executive in the retail and textile industry, Arthur had big dreams and had begun his journey as an entrepreneur. The timing and temperature of the country was right. President Mbeki's leadership inspired a brand of intellectualism and excellence that led us to embody pride in our Africanness. We had a stake and a place in the expansive project towards building a better country, and indeed a better African continent.

I was lured by Arthur's originality, charm, confidence, worldliness, unconventional brand of intellectualism, boundless optimism, expansive body of knowledge, depth of wisdom, adaptability in any setting, gentlemanly manners and generosity. He was the perfect balance between risk and safety. Home and adventure. Observing him take gentle care of little Rhandzo made me fall deeper in love with him. We became a trio, and I opened my heart wide to loving a child I did not birth.

I had met my soulmate. We did things our way. We maintained our separate homes and felt no pressure to rush into nuptials. We excelled at lulling the noise around us.

Despite our combined decisiveness, I was ordered by Tale and Babam to move back to my parental home towards the end of my pregnancy. This is how things were done, we were told. I had purchased and lived in my own home for the past three years. I was firmly and utterly independent. I had my sights on taking up a Public Healthcare Master's degree at Georgetown University in

A MOTHER IS BORN

Washington. I had applied in 2006 and was accepted to commence studies in 2008.

Life had its own agenda, because I gave birth to our first daughter, Ntsumi Ntsako, in January 2007. To my mind, the raising of our daughter would be our exclusive terrain. It turned out we were somewhat ignorant, given that our precious Ntsumi occupied a particular place and position in the lives of her grandparents. Ntsumi was the first grandchild of Tale and Babam and the first granddaughter of Mapule Ruth Mabasa – Arthur's mother.

The fact that I was an admitted attorney of the High Court, on the brink of promotion to partner and a homeowner in a committed relationship had no bearing or relevance on the cultural rite of passage that our mothers knew we had to pass through.

The moment her tiny 3-kilogram and 48-centimetre body was placed onto my chest, I wept internally. Time stopped. Our eyes locked in a gaze that felt like forever. We recognised each other and had longed to finally meet. I felt healed. Healed from known and unknown past hurts and pain. The moment I laid eyes on her, I finally accepted myself. I was afforded a new perspective.

The sky loomed larger, the sun shone brighter and the trees were taller. Where I was weak, I was to make sure my child would gain strength. Where I faltered, she was going to be empowered. Where I failed to see value in myself, she would feel her worth.

When Ntsumi's paternal grandmother Mapule arrived at my parental home, together with Sylvia and Caroline, Arthur's sisters, I keenly observed that Tale handed her the cord stump contained in a white envelope that has fallen off days before.

I had no choice but to accept and embrace the sanctity of those first three months of postpartum motherhood. Being led by Mawe felt right. I appreciated the value, wisdom and intelligence of the ways of my forefathers in rearing a new baby.

Obedience did not come naturally to me, and neither to Arthur. Both Tale and Mapule secretly chuckled and teased their 'highly educated' daughter and son who were so Westernised that they could only gain knowledge when it apppeared in a written text.

Becoming Ntsumi's mother shortly after my 27th birthday humbled me. I was introduced to being, as opposed to doing. I was forced to slow down. Be present. And allow myself to be carried.

28

Partnership

Driving into the office parking lot in the middle of Johannesburg's winter, I felt different. I was no longer alone. I carried my baby's hopes and dreams on my shoulders. I was anchored by Tale, Mawe and Mme. I was intent on elevating my name in the firm and perhaps even beyond. I appreciated and valued the support, guidance and time I had been gifted by Mervyn, Chris, Neil and the rest of the partnership. I needed to craft my own path.

My return from maternity leave coincided with the year I was eligible for promotion to partner. I hoped the five years I had spent committed not only to the firm but also to my own growth would weigh more than the five months I had spent away on maternity leave. Despite the natural worry, I felt I was sharpened, both as a woman and as a lawyer. Of the twelve candidate attorneys who began articles in 2002, I was one of four lawyers promoted to partner.

'*The room was unanimous. Your promotion is well deserved, welcome to hell!*' exclaimed Neil, true to his humour. The outcome humbled me. It spoke of an institution that chose me – all of me, in my fullness of being. In that moment, Werksmans ceased being a mere corporate animal. In my eyes, I was humanised and so was my firm.

Typical in an attorney's practice is not knowing what matter will land on your desk at any given time and what each day would look like. The matters are varied and broad. The intrigue and challenge involve being creative and committed enough to craft a viable, arguable strategy for a client.

A week into my return to the office, I was confronted with a file that would absorb and consume me. It was for the Nkosi family, and Alex Nkosi was the contact person. His mother was a descendant and daughter of the late Phillip Sphezi Nkosi, who hailed from Swaziland and settled in Nelspruit in the 1930s.

Alex's aunt, Rose Ntongolozane Nkosi, had lodged a land claim on behalf of Sphezi's direct descendants. The Nkosi family wanted the restoration of land that Sphezi was dispossessed of because of apartheid laws.

It was as if this file had magnetic powers. I had never dealt with a matter like this before. I slowed down and carefully read the file, finding maps of the lost land and a photograph of Queen Elizabeth, who had visited there in the 1950s and was received by none other than Phillip Sphezi. At the time, Sphezi was a polygamist with six wives.

Despite the Nkosi land claim being submitted timeously in terms of the Restitution of Land Rights Act No. 22 of 2004, it was not investigated by the Commission on the Restitution of Land Rights (often referred to as the Land Claims Commission) and, worse, the claimed land had been awarded to a different family.

It felt as though my entire being, upbringing, legal studies, persuasions and ancestors sent this file my way. It ceased being a client file. It became a calling. The contents of the file stayed with me long after I had bathed Ntsumi and tucked her in.

The typical Werksmans client is a captain of industry, a leading corporate, a mine, a bank, a medical scheme, a hospital, a supplier of goods and services or a listed commercial entity, all invariably led and dominated by white, middle-aged men. This case was different.

The voice on the phone from reception was apprehensive: '*Buls, your clients are here ... quite a few of them ... you will definitely need a bigger boardroom.*'

There were no less than ten representatives of the Nkosi family in the boardroom. I instantly felt at home. It was as if my heritage had met my profession.

Within five minutes, it became counter-intuitive to continue holding the consultation in English. Babu Cain opened the meeting with a prayer in siSwati. This was certainly not how we did things around here, but this was how things were done in Tata's home. This case needed me to present my Africanness. I saw Mawe and Tata in the faces of those present. I knew that this was much bigger than me.

Economics and financial muscle determine who our clients are. The Nkosi family was prepared. They had collected funds from family members to run the case.

After many sleepless nights, incessant breastfeeding and reading up on case law, I was able to devise a legal strategy that would see the Nkosi land claim recognised and subsequently published in the *Government Gazette*. This meant that the Land Claims Commission could no longer ignore the Nkosis' claim.

HERITAGE MEETS PROFESSION

In this area of law, I did not have a mentor, a champion or a teacher. It meant that for the first time in my career as an attorney, I needed to be ahead of the law in many ways.

The process involved countless inspections of the site in Mpumalanga and an assessment of the surrounding graves, including Sphezi's grave and those of his wives. It is impossible for me to forget one such trip that was attended by the elders of Sphezi's descendants and some officials from the Land Claims Commission. I was sitting next to one of Sphezi's daughters under a large baobab tree, overlooking the lush plantations. She turned her beautiful, wrinkled face to me and said: '*Mntanam mhlazane umhlaba wethu ulethwa, siyohlinza, sijabule. Ungedinwa.*'

Mama Nkosi had officially placed on me the massive responsibility of ensuring that the land of her ancestors would be returned. Her words landed on me like a prayer. A plea.

An aspect that slows down the restitution of land processes is a structural one. Land claimant families and communities are typically persons who are indigent or without boundless means. Landowners are often highly resourced and have access to skilled legal professionals to challenge and object to land claims in cases that may take years to resolve. As well-intentioned as the legislation is, its underbelly is fraught with a post-democratic society that is unequal and mired in poverty and unemployment. The result is that even with an enabling law that stands to deliver restorative justice, woven into it is the stubborn legacy of apartheid that continues to permeate every area of social and economic life in the country.

Fifteen years after my first consultation with the Nkosi family, there lies a glimmer of hope. With co-operation from officials at the Land Claims Commission, the landowner, the opposing land claimant family and the Nkosi family, a settlement agreement was reached among the parties.

In the middle of running the Sphezi case, David Hertz called me into his office. His client was the owner of a travel agency and a high-end lodge in Mpumalanga. The client had been running the lodge for many years, and his clientele were mainly international tourists from Europe. The piece of land on which the lodge lay was nestled amid an enchanting forest. The Manzimhlophe community had submitted a claim for the land. In terms of the Restitution Act, a landowner in the position of our client could either object or accept the validity of the claim. Most landowners almost always object, and the Land Claims Commission tries to mediate between the claimants and the owner to resolve the matter. The mediation process can take many years. If it is not possible to reach a settlement, the case is referred to the Land Claims Court. This process also takes years to finalise, with the possibility of further appeals to the Supreme Court of Appeal and to the Constitutional Court.

The Manzimhlophe community case was an anomaly. Here, we had a landowner who understood and accepted the need for land restitution. He did not object, oppose or litigate over the veracity of the land claim made by the community. He was willing and happy to sell the land to the state as provided for in the Restitution Act. The scheme of restitution of land in South Africa is such that once a land claim is lodged, investigated, verified and awarded, it is the state that bears the onus of purchasing the land from the landowner on behalf of the land claimants. The parties also negotiate and ultimately agree on the purchase price payable to the landowner in lieu of the claimed land. Each party is entitled to conduct independent valuations of the land. This was before valuations for land transactions were entrusted to the Office of the Valuer-General. This meant that my client and the Commission would produce their own valuations and negotiate and agree on a purchase price. If no agreement was reached on price, the impasse could be resolved only by a court of law. This is another layer in the restitution process that further delays the settlement of land claims. It is notoriously litigious.

In our case, our client agreed to sell his land and property at a price that was significantly less than market value. He had a vision. Having benefited from years of reaping the rewards of the land through the business of the lodge, he envisioned the internationally acclaimed lodge being operated by the land claimant community, who would not only be employed in the operations, but they would also take charge of the business as equity owners after the settlement of the claim. I was pleasantly surprised. This was a land claim that included the typical characters – a white, well-off landowner and black, dispossessed community – who were ordinarily not expected to see eye to eye.

Unsurprisingly, interactions between land claimants and landowners are riddled with mistrust. In this case, once the community members did not feel spoken for or spoken down to, but duly and properly engaged and consulted in a meaningful manner, I witnessed them responding to the possibilities that lay ahead. They keenly understood that the value was not in the land itself, but it was in the income-generation of the lodge. The land was important,

PARTNERSHIP

but without a cogent and solid business plan, financial assistance and post-settlement support, the land itself would be meaningless. My client went beyond expectations and prepared various business models, all of which were geared towards ultimately ensuring that the community members were able to continue the operation of the lodge independently, long after the landowner had left the business. All the parties were on board.

This matter presented a unique opportunity and a case study that demonstrated that it was indeed possible and feasible to have successful land claim awards that led to sustainable enterprises and operations for a future South Africa. The promise that awaited the Manzimhlophe community was not only that the land of their forefathers would be restored to them, but also that their dignity would be restored as economically active citizens.

The land was successfully purchased by the state on behalf of the community. It was also agreed that our client would remain on the property for a further three years, during which he would train and upskill various members of the community to run the business. This, to me, was a win-win situation.

Feeling confident, I was certain that a post-settlement deal would be reached. I arrived at the Land Claims Commission boardroom with my clients. The relevant Commission officials keenly waited at the opposite end of the table. The Commission was the only party whose signature would be required to finalise the community's vision. If this meeting lasted longer than 30 minutes, it was too long.

'Our role is to return the land to the people. We have now done that. We have no business assisting the community with any post-settlement

support, be it business plans or whatever. Our job is done.' These words were uttered by a senior member of the Department of Land Affairs. I was gobsmacked. It felt like a kick in my stomach. The Manzimhlophe community had been awarded their land back without the wherewithal of how to use it for productive future purposes. Within twelve months of the land having been awarded, the buildings were derelict, abandoned and hollowed out. The Manzimhlophe community was left worse off than it had been before the land claim was finalised.

It dawned on me that the Restitution Act has a glaring and serious omission: it places no legal obligation on the Commission to care about, plan for and provide resources that will ensure that once a land claim is awarded, the claimants are not set up for failure. I published a variety of articles in the media, galvanising and advocating for a possible amendment of the Restitution Act to address this legal lacuna. As it stands, adequate, meaningful, post-settlement support remains an elusive concept in restitution that lingers in unclear, internal policies of the Department of Land Affairs.

29

Independence

I was bursting to carve out my own path. It was time to sharpen my administrative and constitutional law skills that I had learned in Neil's practice.

'*Thank you for agreeing to see me. I need your support as the head of litigation. I am ready to build my own practice, and I am going to need your help.*' It took me about a week before I built up the chutzpah to approach David Hertz. I did not know what to expect. But I knew one thing: I had to speak with conviction and be pointed and brief in my delivery. To my surprise, he paused and said: '*Right, you have my support, do not disappoint.*'

A day after the meeting, David called me into his office. '*Here, go run with this.*' It was a blue-chip client in the metal-recycling industry. The company had lost a tender bid to collect scrap metal from Eskom. The tender was awarded to an entity that had no track record in that industry. In fact, the entity had submitted its bid relying not on its own financial statements but on those of another entity. I was particularly interested in the public procurement of goods and services by the state, given this was in line with my experience and interest in administrative and constitutional law. Gifted with great instincts, David knew exactly the type of case that would pique my interest.

I took extra care in the matter, knowing that it would determine how trusted I would be as an attorney single-handedly taking on Eskom in a political environment where state procurement was viewed with suspicion. The case was adjudicated in the High Court and argued successfully by counsel. We also succeeded on appeal in the Supreme Court of Appeal. The effect of the review of the tender was that Eskom was ordered to commence afresh the process of appointing a bidder lawfully.

The procurement of goods and services by the state soon became the hallmark of my budding practice. I had begun writing opinion pieces in news publications and became a regular commentator on radio shows, shining a spotlight on the dangers, challenges and possible abuses in the manner in which the state made decisions on who to procure goods and services from. It became clear to me that, left unchecked, state procurement had the potential to collapse the country.

Soon after the High Court and Supreme Court of Appeal victories, I received a call from my colleague and partner Elliott Wood. He was referring a matter to me that he thought was appropriate for my skill set. It was another case involving the state procurement of goods and services. This time, it was a national tender for the provision of catering services to all the prisons in the country.

My client was an entity that had been informed of a suspicious and unsavoury relationship between the officials of the Department of Correctional Services and a company that was awarded the tender. All we had been informed of at that stage was the fact that department officials were given benefits in the form of free rugby tickets and stationery. My client was a competitor of the winning bidder. The client felt that it was unduly denied the opportunity to tender fairly and in a transparent manner. When the entity was informed that it was unsuccessful in its tender bid, the reason it was given was that it failed to include a bank guarantee in its bid. But my client kept a duplicate copy of the submitted bid. Something untoward had happened. Its tender submission was deliberately tampered with to make room for whatever entity the department wanted to award the tender to.

This case intrigued me. I was struck by how Section 217 of the Constitution – the purpose of which is to direct the state to procure goods and services in an open, fair, transparent, cost-effective and competitive manner – could easily be manipulated by anyone with contrary intent.

It became evident to me that the decisions being made by state officials on which entity would be awarded a state contract to buy stationery, toilet paper or provide sidewalk grass-cutting were as important as the decisions being made about which company would be the best placed to build stadiums, power stations, roads and hospitals.

Our opponent was Bosasa. Unbeknown to me, an innocuous matter that could easily have been regarded as a commercial matter, where competitors were warring over which party deserved a lion's share of doing business with the public sector, would a decade later bring to the fore the rise of endemic corruption and patronage that has dominated much of post-democratic South Africa.

Soon into the matter, the national catering tender awarded to Bosasa ceased being a simple legal instruction that advanced my administrative and constitutional skills. It dominated newspaper publications and headlines. I was successful in having Bosasa's tender reviewed and set aside by the Pretoria High Court. We obtained the judgment three years after the hearing. By the time the judgment was delivered, there were only a few months left on the contract. The setting aside of the tender could not be implemented given the time that had lapsed between the filing of the matter and the delivery of the judgment. We had written various letters of complaint to the Judicial Service Commission about the inordinately late delivery of the judgment, but they fell on deaf ears. I had learned a sobering lesson: law and justice are not synonymous. It was a legal victory, but with little justice.

Soon after the Bosasa catering tender, more cases followed on tender disputes, including the setting aside of decisions by the Minister of Minerals and Energy on the award of mineral rights licences.

Before I knew it, I had been able to garner a sustainable practice that was not only profitable but also shaped and anchored by my love of constitutional law and social justice.

30

The Quest for Social Impact and Meaning

I felt a deep connection between the work I woke up to do every day and how it affected the person on the street. I knew that it was not enough for me to be locked in my office drafting. It was time to gather the courage to bring it to the public domain.

Having had the benefit and experience of seeing how Neil kept abreast of legislative and policy changes in healthcare and finding ways in which the law made its way to newspaper articles, television interviews and professional publications, I knew what was possible. I began writing articles about the flaws in the public tendering system, commented on legislative changes and said 'yes' to any and every radio and television opportunity to air my views.

Perhaps the most significant encounter in the public sphere was when I was invited to the Radio 702 studios. Redi Tlhabi had come across my name in various media articles in relation to state tendering, and my work caught her eye. I benefited from her morning show's widespread listenership, and this culminated in me being invited by the station to host a weekly slot called *A Word on Legal Matters*.

Every time I walked into the studio I hoped and prayed that I would not bungle a question on an area of law I knew nothing about. When I left the studio, I felt massively relieved. After my first show, a plethora of messages of congratulations and well-wishes flooded my phone. Most did not even comment on the content of the show; people were simply elated that I – someone they knew, worked with or had been to school with – occupied that space. Many more were strangers. I had a voice and I used it.

I did not do this blindly and without preparation. I was blessed with an opportunity to attend media training sessions with none other than Bruce Whitfield, role-playing possible disastrous scenarios. I learned the importance of ensuring I had three key messages to leave my audiences with and ways in which I could use the media platform to advance my own predetermined messages.

An opportunity arose to do a television show with Redi, which kept me connected with what ordinary South Africans were grappling with and what they perceived the law could do for them. Many viewers' issues were concentrated on land and housing, rental disputes and illegal evictions. I came to realise that our law had not developed to a point where a person living in an informal settlement or a backyard room could fully utilise the law to seek justice.

Our laws are still heavily influenced by Roman-Dutch law, which is skewed in favour of those who operate within the formal property law system, with lease agreements, title deeds, notarial bonds and registered servitudes. It was on this television show that I fully appreciated that I was not in a position to adequately provide cogent and legal-based answers to the callers.

There was an entire body of law that was not built to help black and poor people attain secure and legally enforceable land rights. Parliament had done very little to rectify the legacy of apartheid laws. If you were black and poor, you had marginal or no access to land, operated on the periphery of the economy and were doomed to dwell on the sidelines of development.

Although there was no immediate correlation between all the time I spent on 'work' outside the practice and money in the bank, this work fulfilled me. Subconsciously I wanted my voice to matter.

The cracks in the state tendering system were beginning to show. I was particularly bothered by how the noble and necessary principles of Black Economic Empowerment were being bastardised by cronyism and corruption, to the detriment of the economy. I was receiving new matters from multinationals and major companies, which were challenging dubious tender awards involving hundreds of millions, if not billions, of rand.

My passion and the work that paid me met at a confluence.

31

A Tale of Joy and Sorrow

It was a sensational time. Six years into our relationship, Arthur and I decided that we were ready to get married. We had both been working steadily and purposefully on growing our respective careers.

I had cemented my name and value in the firm. In Arthur's eyes, I was a leader waiting to be born. He had experienced first-hand how my cases mattered to me, how I would bring work home and how my eyes lit up or how hurt I would be if I felt that a matter did not go the way that I wanted it to. He saw how my work inhabited my entire being. He did not see the need for me to divide my love for my work and my love for him and our family. To him, all these loves could coexist, and he made sure our lives accommodated my reality.

We had agreed on a date for our nuptials. 30 October. It was our favourite time of the year, with the jacaranda trees in full bloom, perfect blue skies, lush trees and heart-piercing sunsets. It was 2010,

A TALE OF JOY AND SORROW

and it felt like nothing and no one could touch us.

Our countrymen and -women were still intoxicated from the exhilarating energy of the FIFA World Cup, which was hosted on African soil for the first time. It seemed like South Africans could take a moment to escape the clutches of widening inequality, poverty and growing unemployment.

Babam and Tale were thrust deeply into their role as grandparents. Arthur and I moved into our first marital home. We loved to have our family and friends over. Life was truly smiling at us. In the same year, the Khemese family had six weddings in total. Every other weekend felt like a celebration.

Tale, Nomfundo and Ntsumi were a regular trio. They went everywhere together – to church and malls and on visits. My sisters had become grown women, except for Nomfi who was only fifteen.

I was six months pregnant, and we had found out we would be having another girl. We named her Akani Rifumo. To build wealth. I was radiant and active.

I had flown to George to attend the annual Werksmans Directors' Conference, which is a never-to-be-missed annual calendar item.

Ntsumi was four, and she would be spending the weekend with her beloved gogo and Nomfundo at home. '*Mama, here are all the instructions on how and when to administer her meds. I have also included her daily schedule and routine. Oh, no sweets, Ma, you know how she gets.*' I did this as if I was not leaving my slightly sick child behind with the woman who had raised me, and who had been in the medical profession her whole life.

It was the morning of 14 May, and I was attending a conference

HERITAGE MEETS PROFESSION

session that had captivated my attention. I looked down at my watch. It was 9.30 am. I felt an urgent need to find out how the night had gone with Tale, Nomfi and Ntsumi.

I walked out of the seminar room into the lobby and dialled my mother's mobile number. When her phone just rang and rang, I knew something was wrong. I phoned Nani, Fuzi and Zone – all without a response. My last resort was to dial my parents' home number. My hands were trembling. I was relieved when I heard Nomfi's voice on the other end of the phone.

'*Hi, Nomfi. How are you? Where is everyone? I have been trying to get hold of Tale all morning.*'

'*I don't know, Buls, Tale left earlier to buy mealie meal and milk to make some porridge for Ntsumi before she takes her meds. She's been gone a while. Zone left to look for her. Now Nani has also gone to look for her.*' My heart sank. Something had definitely happened.

'*Nomf, where is Ntsumi? Is she with you? Please let me speak to her on the phone. Are you sure she did not leave with Tale?*'

Miraculously, Tale had left home without Nomfundo and Ntsumi on that fateful day. I breathed a sigh of short-lived relief that at least my baby sister and daughter were safely at home.

'*Buls, Arthur is on the line. We have to get you onto the next flight to Joburg. There has been an emergency at home,*' my colleague said, managing to keep her composure. I could no longer hold in the rush of emotion. I still did not know what had happened, but I felt it. Right there in that lobby. Joburg was only two hours away, but those two hours felt like two lifetimes.

'*Buls, there is no way you are stepping onto that plane and doing that trip alone,*' persisted my friend Jacqui Kallmeyer. She and I had studied together and started our articles at the same time at Werksmans. Our paths were inseparable, and our professional life was soon overtaken by a sisterhood. She and her husband Trevor Boswell rallied around me during that flight.

Walking as fast as I could past the conveyer belts and weaving through the crowds at the airport arrivals, I could not wait to read Arthur's face. When our eyes eventually locked, I knew the worst had happened, but I was still hopeful. Hopeful that the woman who carried, nurtured and loved me silly was at least still breathing. I desperately wanted to see and be with my mother.

As we turned into Farnham Drive, I saw the rows of cars on either side of the street. I ran to see what emotion lay in Naniwe's eyes. Just as Arthur had done, she too looked away. She wore a black doek, her eyes were bloodshot and her face was stern. It still did not register as confirmation of the worst.

Fuzi and Zone ran towards me, crying, '*Buls, she is at peace, she is at peace.*' I hated that my little sisters were ushering me into the dark world of the unknown, when it should have been me who did that for them. The silence of the house almost swallowed me up. I looked around, seeking my father's face. I needed to look in his eyes, and when he, too, looked downwards I felt a helplessness I have never experienced before.

'*Sit down, my baby. uTale usishiyile emhlabeni. She is no more. Your mother perished in a car accident this morning.*' Sheila Masote was the family elder tasked with the formal duty of relaying the news to me. My world fell apart.

Babam had also been away, performing at a gig in Durban. We were the last people to know of his beloved's passing. She was not the only person we lost that day. My sisters and I lost our father too. Although he lived for the next five years, Babam's stature, grandeur, strength, guiding force and light were extinguished that day.

When I walked into Fuzi and Zone's room, Arthur was there. It was as if he had been waiting for this moment to share his grief with me. When he had lost his mother, Mapule, two years before, I thought I had grasped the level of his pain. In this moment, however, I was also grieving for how I never fully comprehended his grief for his mother. A year before we wed, I was the one who was tasked by his mother to inform him and his siblings about her deteriorating health. On this day, he was the one at the scene of the car accident with Zone, and he had to be the bearer of bad news. Seven months into our marriage, we both realised the vastness of our responsibilities, not only to our new little family, but also towards our siblings.

Tale's death solidified our sisterly bond. I had to step into my mother's shoes and take on the mother role. I did everything to try to shield my sisters from the pain. It finally dawned on me why my middle name, Sesi, was significant and nothing to be scoffed at. I needed to live up to it and embrace it.

On a bitterly cold day, I gave birth to our Akani Rifumo, exactly three months after we buried Tale. Akani was the baby who brought healing to my heart. As spiritual and ancestral bonds go, it turned out that Mme took her last breath after she enquired about the status of my labour on that day. Mme did not just leave, she gifted us with Akani on the day of her passing.

'*Buli sa kreile ngwana? Ke mosetsana?*' Mme was on the phone with my mother's eldest sister, praying and enquiring whether I had

had a successful delivery. She bowed out when she was certain that Akani and I were healthy. This was her last act of mothering her late daughter. This was the day that I knew that joy and pain could coexist.

Akani was the gift that brought colour and texture back to our lives. With a mysterious but profound presence, it was as if she had been here before and that she knew what she came here to do. She inhabited her name – to rebuild and to spread the wealth of love.

32

Raising Children while Building a Law Practice

Weighing heavily on my mind (and body) was the concern I had about the sustainability and survival of my practice. I feared that a five-month hiatus on maternity leave would send me into a world of obscurity in the minds of my clients. I was on the phone daily and tended to e-mails. My reality was that all my cases were at their peak, requiring various interlocutory applications, hearings and court processes. I had invested my time and expertise in those cases for at least three years prior and I had to remain present and visible and continue taking the lead.

Giving up practice was not on my radar. I reconciled myself with breastfeeding, changing nappies, cuddling and kissing my children by day, and keeping my practice afloat by night. My home became a village. My sisters became deputy mothers to my babies, Arthur mastered the night-shift duty while I tried to get a few hours of sleep, meals were delivered, and my aunts took turns to help during bath time. As complex as my world had become, I had a tremendous support system.

RAISING CHILDREN/BUILDING A PRACTICE

In the midst of all this, I had enrolled in a postgraduate course in prospecting and mining. Mining work seemed to follow me, and I felt it was necessary to bolster my knowledge and skills. My pregnancy did not deter me from attending lectures in the evenings.

It was a pitiful scene, in retrospect. Our marital bed was covered in no less than twenty textbooks, journal articles and law reports. In my nightdress, I would be typing away to hand in an assignment the next day.

'Take it easy, my love. I am here. We will get through this.' Arthur's practical love and acts of service kept me sane and our home fires burning.

When I returned to the office, I became part of the firm's Professional Staff Committee. This is a role in management that is tasked with recruiting, interviewing and hiring future candidate attorneys, and looking after their well-being during their articles. It appealed to me to connect with the younger lawyers and gave me the opportunity to break free from the conservativism of the culture of hierarchy in the legal industry. I could bring to the committee a perspective that cut across the value judgements that human beings often make, shaped by their own prejudices. I could recognise a gaze that was lumbered with an inferiority complex or a trembling hand that smacked of uncertainty and low self-esteem. I was keenly aware of the non-verbal and verbal messages I had received when interviewing at other law firms a decade earlier. The face of a law firm of the future had to be diverse and inclusive.

I legitimately felt like an all-rounder. I had finally found a rhythm I was happy with.

'Love, the only time you vomit like this is when you're pregnant,' Arthur

said casually as he threw the used towels into the washing basket. My mind started racing. It had only been eight months since I had returned from maternity leave. I could not be!

33

Crown of the Nation

I could not wait to share the news with Babam. He had become frail and purposeless. Life without Tale depleted his essence. He had become a recluse, retreating to his bedroom and listening to the soft, melancholic sounds of classical music.

The doctor confirmed at our twenty-week check-up: '*The sex of this baby is not changing, Mrs Mabasa … This is definitely a boy.*' I was ecstatic. As proud as Babam had been of his five girls, I could not wait to share the news of his expected first grandson.

We named him Harhi Rixaka. Crown of the Nation. '*He looks exactly like his sisters,*' Arthur swooned, as he held his moist, tiny body against his chest.

Babam's healing was assisted by his grandchildren. He shared a particularly strong bond with Rixaka. The doting grandfather role suited him and warmed my heart. He regained his mischievous giggle, dry sense of humour and his penchant for goodies and spoils.

Despite my concern about his ill health and that I felt he was not fully equipped to chaperone the kids to and from school, I was proven wrong each time. His ailing body did not reflect the strength and growth of his spirituality. '*Mommy, Khulu gave us homework. We have to read and memorise Psalm 23. Look, Khulu gave us our own Bibles.*' His spiritual prowess was at its peak, and I discovered I had never lost my father after all.

The first five years of being a partner at the firm coincided with the years that I birthed my three children. Arthur took on much of what would have fallen on my shoulders, making a way for me to deal with the business of the day. He did the school trips and doctors' appointments with grace. As much as I was able to enlist family support, I felt that only I could be a mother to my children. My practice slowed down. I had fewer billable hours. I was acutely aware that my children's formative years formed a crucial base for their future lives. There would be no second take.

Naively, it did not quite register with me that the decision I made to be a present mother while being a lawyer and partner in the firm was a decision to forgo a part of my earnings. I was blindsided when I saw the allocations table. My baby-producing abilities became career-limiting. Given the choice again, I would make the same decision without a doubt. It was not lost on me that the firm afforded me the opportunity to be flexible in how I worked, where I worked and for how long.

I was sitting next to a partner at a lunch table, and we were enjoying some light banter. He muttered the following words while piercing his lamb chop with his knife: '*I don't know what I would do without my wife. She runs our household and makes it possible for me for me to run my practice.*' His statement hit me in the most unexpected but telling way.

PART 5

Of Land and Ancestors

34

A Land Reform Practice Takes Root

In 2011, South Africa hosted the United Nations Climate Change Conference in Durban. Subsequently, the Renewable Energy Independent Power Producer Programme was introduced in the country, which was aimed at building a green economy and moving away from the more traditional fossil-powered modes of producing electricity. Government invited private-sector players to submit competitive bids for the supply of solar, wind and hydro energy. This initiative was imperative for the growth of new industries and as a way to create much-needed jobs. I enrolled at the Mandela Institute to take a course in energy law to service any clients wanting to participate in this area.

I was approached by colleagues in our commercial department who were representing two of the preferred bidders for the construction of photovoltaic solar farms. One of the project owners needed to secure land for the building of the Witkop solar farm in Limpopo Province. It transpired that a community had submitted a claim on the land. The main funders of the project were uncertain about whether the existence of a land claim posed a risk. The challenge for me was to ascertain whether it was possible for the funding of the project to continue amid the existence of a land claim.

This case crystallised for me in fundamental and practical ways how land reform dwelled on the periphery, almost an outpost located away from the formal economy. The country's need to diversify its energy mix and the community's constitutional right to have its land restored were both key national objectives that were presented to me, as if they competed. In a country riddled with widening inequality, joblessness and an unreliable electricity supply, the investment in renewable energy was desperately needed. The community's desire to have its land restored was not only a financial necessity, but also a way of reviving its dignity, stake and belonging in a country that had excluded the community and its ancestors for centuries. To my mind, both were nationally significant imperatives.

The first challenge was to demystify the idea that land restitution, in and of itself, was antithetical to development and economic growth. My job was to shift the funders' mindset, which was largely informed by fear and mistrust of land reform, and to demonstrate that it was their constitutional obligation to embrace land reform as part of their business strategy.

In my opinion, the two objectives were not mutually exclusive. It became my personal mission. As far as I was concerned, the issues were clear in law. If the land claim was found to be valid, then the community would act as landowner and landlord in a lease agreement, with the project company being the tenant. My mind extended to a place of further possibilities, where community members could form part of the project, gain valuable skills and even become part-owners. The drafting of the terms and conditions of a lease agreement, with the relevant resolutive conditions in place, was the easiest part.

More challenging was bringing to light the intricacies of the Constitution, the Restitution Act and the Expropriation Act. The fear of expropriation was palpable. My role was to outline and simplify the applicable laws and to delineate them beyond the bounds of the dominant narrative that was perpetuated by the mainstream media. What hogged the headlines was the idea that land reform, and expropriation in particular, would dissuade economic investment and collapse the economy.

It is no wonder then that what I viewed to be innocuous principles around land reform were believed to be catastrophic. This was an exercise in converting those responsible for making funding decisions to embrace the notion that economic activity and investment were not threatened by restoring land to its rightful owners. Although it took many months to convince various committees, in the end the investors agreed to fund the project, with the possibility that one day the land might be awarded to the community.

Soon thereafter, I was approached by a client who was in the process of constructing a new hospital in Nelspruit. The land on which the hospital was being built was under a community land claim, which was being investigated by the Commission on the Restitution of Land Rights. The client's fear was based on a false narrative that the Commission had to consent to the project, when legally the client simply had to notify the Commission. I was again taken aback by the dearth of information in this area in matters that involved major capital outlay. This aspect alone had the potential of derailing the entire project. It would have been a travesty to halt the construction of a hospital in an area that was in dire need because of a statutory provision that was seemingly unfamiliar to the professionals involved. Ultimately, through my intervention with the officials at the Commission, the hospital was built and the fear that a land claim could not coexist with a commercial development was abated.

35

Rebuilding

Over and above my interest in state procurement and administrative and constitutional law, I set my sights on introducing a Land Reform, Restitution and Tenure practice area at Werksmans. When I looked at the other four of the Big-Five law firms, I realised that none of them had a dedicated practice area in land reform. The Big-Five firms typically service the corporate, financial, mining and services sectors. The lodgement or the defence of land claims, objections to land claims, litigating before the Land Claims Court, dealing with the Commission on the Restitution of Land Rights, expropriation claims, expropriation litigation and the like were not considered to be matters that were linked to or impacted by the main economy.

'David, I have decided. Land reform is one burning issue that is not going away anytime soon. None of our competitors have placed any particular focus on it as a stand-alone practice area. I am ready to spearhead it. I have done my homework. I have the practical experience.' My conviction was unquestionable. I was not asking for permission.

'Go for it! You have my full support. Name anything and everything you *need. It is a done deal.*' I knew I had overprepared for our meeting, but I had not anticipated that David would instantly buy into my vision. He saw it. The nod from the top gave me the impetus and courage I needed to forge ahead.

I had decided that the practice would be more than simply a conduit for land reform cases. It was going to bring land reform issues decidedly into the public domain. It would serve to inform, invoke debate and contribute to why land reform remained a constitutional promise that the stability and future of the country was hinged on.

It was twenty years since South Africa's first democratic election in 1994. It was a significant year on many fronts. It was President Jacob Zuma's final year of his first term. South Africa was gearing up for a general election in May that year, and the ANC was showing clear divisions within the party, exemplified mainly by the firing of its youth leader, Julius Malema. This was also the first election that the country would be holding after the death of Nelson Mandela. The Economic Freedom Fighters (EFF) had just been formed, led by Malema, and its ideology was hinged on the nationalisation of land in South Africa.

Government had admitted to having been woefully slow to meet its target of redistributing 30 per cent of land to black people by 2014. This target was focused on the redistribution of agricultural farmland belonging to white commercial farmers. Widening poverty, unemployment and inequality heavily influenced the trend of land claimants opting for financial compensation instead of the return of their lost land.

Perhaps more significantly, this was the year in which President Zuma made an announcement that the date on which land claims could be lodged was to be extended from 31 December 1998 to 20 June 2014, and the Khoi and San people would be able to lay land claims even if the dispossession took place prior to 19 June 1913. The plan to reopen the lodgement of new land claims was touted amid an overwhelming backlog of over 30 000 claims that had not been finalised or settled.

My practice was overflowing with queries from existing and prospective clients who were community and family land claimants, prospective land claimants, farmers, banks, mining companies and mining communities.

In the same year, the Department of Rural Development and Land Reform issued land reform-related Bills that added to the uncertainty – the Regulation of Agricultural Land Holdings Bill and the Restitution of Land Rights Amendment Bill. These Bills were touted as attempts to fast-track and accelerate the slow pace of land reform. The Land Holdings Bill included, among other things, the state's attempt to compel current landowners to disclose their racial make-up, the creation of a public land register and the prohibition of ownership of land by foreigners. The Restitution Bill sought to extend the deadline for the submission of land claims.

The political climate, the impending changes in the land reform arena and my personal goals for my land reform practice had converged. The time was right.

36

Media Exposure

Before I knew it, my voice and pen were dominating the relevant publications, both professional and public. My mobile phone did not stop ringing. My voice and opinions mattered across media platforms.

I worked closely with our internal marketing team, and together we sought out every opportunity to profile my name and my practice. I was intentional about which segments of society I was aiming for. Newspaper headlines were latching onto the extreme positions of the left- and right-wing political parties. Politicians used land reform as political football and a means to sow further division. Few played the role of a voice of reason. South Africans needed clarity.

I felt at ease in front of the camera and before a microphone. I relived the feeling I had had when I was first in a studio at four years old. I ensured that I was prepared for every radio or television interview, but invariably my passion took over. It was contained passion. I had an acute awareness that although the practice area was very politically and emotionally charged, I was never the subject.

MEDIA EXPOSURE

I was the vessel to distil the law, to tackle it when it needed to be challenged and to diagnose the shortcomings but never without a solution.

To me, the man and woman on the street had the right not only to be informed but also to hold accountable those entrusted to deliver its objectives.

I had to keep my knowledge current. I received invitations to debunk, analyse and clarify key developments. I used every interview and article as a way to spread a message that land reform was necessary and urgent, and our unified hopes and future stability of the country were woven into it.

37

Saving a Sacred Seat for the Ancestors

Sometimes the highlight in the day of a life of an attorney is a shared meal with a colleague. David was sitting opposite me. *'I've just had the most fascinating consultation. Do you know anything about spiritual and cultural rights?'* I sat up immediately. *'I'm your person, assign this case to me.'*

Earlier, David had consulted with a group of environmentalists, game-reserve owners, farmers and landowners. They were deeply concerned about an Australian-owned mine that had recently and unlawfully begun operating on a mountain known locally as the Meletse mountain. The landowners and the community had expressed their concerns and unhappiness about the possibility of Meletse mountain being desecrated by the iron-ore mine. During the consultation, one of the landowners indicated that he had heard from his housekeeper that the threatened mountain 'inhabits the spirits of our ancestors'.

The next consultation took place in a large boardroom, with

SAVING A SACRED SEAT FOR THE ANCESTORS

ten seats occupied by concerned community members. The mining company had unlawfully destroyed trees and built more roads than it was permitted. Beyond the obvious legal transgressions that emanated under mining and environmental law, I could not unhear the words: '*This is the seat of our ancestors.*'

I was careful about remaining objective and single-minded about the mission ahead. It was not for me to invent a course of action for the community of Meletse. Rather, this was an investigative, exploratory and learning process, in which I needed to allow myself to be teachable and malleable.

My place as a Western-trained practising attorney could not lull my grounding as an African woman. The perspective and depth that I was bringing to the table were my lived experience and deep connection with the notion that our ancestors communicate with us in various dimensions. This case presented an opportunity to delve meaningfully into the significance of land not for its finite and patrimonial uses, not for its economic or financial value, but for its ability to heal people and to remind them of who they are and where they come from.

The mission to defend the Meletse mountain had several legally sound bases. The mining company was clearly in contravention of the environmental and mining prescripts of the country. It did not have a mining right awarded to it, nor did it have any environmental authorisation. Notionally and legally, we could have stopped there. But something about the mysterious claims of the spiritual and cultural significance of the case stood out for our team.

We travelled to Meletse to experience it ourselves. We eventually arrived at a homestead adjacent to the imposing mountain. We waited behind the chicken-wire gate before it was opened for us. We were met by a dark-skinned man with the widest smile. His athletic stature stood in contrast to his obvious age. His red-tinged eyes and wrinkles told the story of someone who had spent his life labouring under the unforgiving African sun.

'*Dumelang bana baka, tsenang. O bolelang ke Thomas Mothloki.*' I felt a heightened sense of familiarity. It was as if I had been here before. Ntate Mothloki could easily have been one of my relatives in Marapyane. With each footstep I took in the red soil, I felt that this moment was intrisically predetermined. Time stopped as we hung on to each word that Ntate Mothloki uttered as he related his family and descendants' attachment and connection to Meletse mountain and the cave.

He was born and bred on this land. To the indigenous people of this community, the land was known as Madimatle. Beautiful Blood. His eyes sparkled as he explained the significance of Madimatle not only to him personally but also to the entire community. I pictured him as a growing boy, playing in the expansive, rocky but lush vegetation and herding cows along the pretty streams. He described his childhood experience and life as a young man, with Madimatle serving as the majectic, mystical foundation for his people's sense of being, heritage and identity. His wife shared similar sentiments as she gazed melancholically into the distance.

According to the Mothlokis, Madimatle is an integration of the Madimatle mountain and a nearby cave, which form interconnected spiritual and cultural shrines. For the Bakgatla ba Mocha, Madimatle represented a place of refuge and a battleground of the Tswana warriors who fought wars and battles with the Boers and during the

Mfecane era. Madimatle was the final resting place of his ancestors who fought to keep their land. This was the lineage that both my maternal and paternal grandmothers came from.

We later met with one of the landowners in the area. He was a tall and burly man with a gentle heart. We walked into his home, where his young housekeeper greeted us. When she had heard about the threat of mining and the possibility that Madimatle may be desecrated, she apparently retorted: '*It is impossible. Badimo would never allow mining to happen there. This is a very sacred and important mountain to my people.*' Her mother had suffered ill health and had received a message through dreams to seek prayer and healing at Madimatle. She later found out that she had an ancestral calling to be an *ngaka*, a healer. Madimatle was where her mother underwent initiation as a traditional healer, and the shrine from where she would *phahla*.

We drove on the bumpy and dusty road that led to an impounded area with a locked gate and a sign that restricts access to the Madimatle cave. The mining company was effectively prohibiting the people of Madimatle from exercising their right to practise their culture and spirituality.

As we looked through the gate into the cave, I felt a pronounced sense of urgency to assist the people of Madimatle.

38

Spirits Don't Cower

The more I researched and read about Madimatle, the more it revealed its layers to me. I came across writings and books on its spiritual, religious and cultural fortitude. I discovered that Madimatle had been significant during the Iron Age, with iron found and used for weapons and farming. I recalled reading about the mountains of Thabazimbi in Credo Mutwa's *Indaba, My Children*. I embarked on a mission to find him. I eventually stumbled on a mobile number and was able to contact him. I was electrified. The acclaimed author, *isanusi* and holder of African mythology and wisdom extraordinaire, Babu Mutwa, agreed to speak to me about Madimatle.

He listened attentively on the phone as I relayed the essence of my case. He knew immediately about Madimatle. He was dejected and sorrowful about what he termed 'a relentless effort at the erasure of our heritage and culture by destroying our sacred sites'. Babu Mutwa claimed that the final way to conquer Africans was in their sense of being and their spiritual prowess. His despondent tone was intertwined with audible pain. My objective was to meet with him and his wife in person in Kuruman. He declined.

I consulted the Traditional Healers Organisation, which has over 39 000 members under its banner. I met with the Kara Heritage Institute. I was left unwavering in the assertion that Madimatle was worthy of protection.

I followed up with a second visit to the Traditional Healers Organisation. The national co-ordinator, Phephisile Maseko, knew of hundreds of members of the organisation who were routine visitors to Madimatle. We spent a day engaging with, interviewing and taking down statements from many people who practised as traditional healers in order to capture their lived experiences and connection to Madimatle.

A highlight of this visit was meeting Gogo Grace Masuku at one of the community library buildings she had assisted in constructing. Refusing to allow her age to deter her independence and sense of purpose, she was still driving herself everywhere in her vintage Range Rover. As she took us around her community vegetable gardens, stopping to chuckle, dish out a word or two of advice and loving and living for her community, I witnessed her true essence as an environmentalist, teacher and philanthropist. She articulated with aplomb the journey of the Bakgatla people and their connection to Madimatle. In the community hall, we listened to how a mountain and a cave had healed scores of people from all over, how people from all walks of life regularly travelled to the mountain and cave to connect with their ancestors and reclaim missing parts of who they are.

The next day we made our way to Madimatle. It was a Sunday. Stunned by the number of cars, taxis and vans that encircled the entrance to the cave, we spotted groups of worshippers in various church uniforms. What I was seeing play out in front of me was borne out by the literature I had engaged. The only thing left for me to do was to express all that I had witnessed and been intrigued by into a plausible legal remedy to save the Madimatle mountain and cave.

The National Heritage Resources Act provided a useful remedy to have the mountain and cave protected and declared heritage sites. Our research and grounding were solid and compelling enough for us to conclude that it should form part of a national estate that is worthy of protection. The Constitution held a promise to the people of Madimatle that it was not a hollow instrument that is lauded internationally, but one that would clothe itself in the land of the people of its birth.

Over the next seven years, rigorous litigation ensued. Multiple challenges were meted against the mining company's environmental and mining processes.

If ever there was any truth in what Ntate Mothloki had said, he was right. The spirits of the Bakgatla ancestors would never cower.

Fighting a noble and just cause, such as the Madimatle case, requires considerable financial resources. This was a battle that involved giant law firms with experienced and capable lawyers on both sides. The answers were far from simple. Our opponents were arguing for an open-cast iron-ore mine that would employ 400 people from the local community for a period of eighteen years. We were arguing for the sustainability of the enviromental, anthropological, historical, paleontological, traditional and cultural preservation of land and heritage resources that held tangible and intangible qualities, which money, time and space could not quantify.

There was a lack of an overarching government policy and national direction to guide the intersection of rights between mining and development, on the one hand, and the need to protect our natural and heritage resources, on the other. In other words, there is no system of prioritisation of land uses over others, and no ultimate decider. The Madimatle case is still underway and will be determinative of the balancing of constitutional rights, the freedom to practise culture and religion, and the right to free trade.

39

Recognising, Protecting and Supporting Indigenous Knowledge Systems

The need and struggle for land and land justice are not always about its financial value, nor is it about asserting patrimonial interests by an individual or a corporation. For many in rural South Africa, it is attached to a sense of shared identity, collective cultural expression and generational heritage.

I was approached by an NGO assisting the chief of the Amahlubi Traditional Council and the community of Ndabakazi in the Eastern Cape. Since time immemorial, their forebears had passed onto them, through oral history and storytelling, how to use and preserve various indigenous medicinal plants that grow organically on their land for healing purposes. The value of land for the people of Ndabakazi is directly and intrinsically connected with their sense of being, survival and healing.

Nontando Ngamlana, the executive director of the NGO,

consulted with me, along with Chief Mvuyiswa Luzipho. Conversing exclusively in isiXhosa, we were to assist the people of Ndabakazi with a fact-finding mission.

The community had discovered that various players had descended on their land and taken a keen interest in two plant species. Chief Luzipho was asked to furnish informed and prior consent for the bioprospecting of the plants, which were to be commercialised and patented by various universities, involving tens of millions of rand. The chief felt he could not purport to act for or to furnish the consent on behalf of the people of Ndabakazi on this matter.

The National Environmental Management: Biodiversity Act 10 of 2004 regulates applicants seeking to use natural products for commercial reasons, and it specifies that an application needs to be made to the Department of Environmental Affairs and Tourism (DEAT) for a permit to allow for commercialisation to take place. I wondered whether the people of Ndabakazi would be recognised and protected in the application process, and if the DEAT has sufficient and adequate safeguards in place to track, monitor, evaluate and ultimately protect the community from any form of exploitation.

The law of bioprospecting indigenous plant and medicinal products sets out that all relevant stakeholders and holders of indigenous knowledge are listed and engaged. It also stipulates that indigenous knowledge holders must consent to the application, and the parties must enter into various agreements to regulate benefits and profit-sharing arrangements, which include any royalty payments due to the indigenous knowledge system holders.

It was imperative that I understood the location of the land on which the plants grew. This seemingly basic enquiry proved to be a challenge. Given that the land in question is located on former TBVC land, it has not been surveyed before. The land has no registered address. We could not obtain GPS co-ordinates. This meant that the Deeds Registry has no record of this land on its system. When I heard for the first time from a colleague and friend who was born and bred in the Eastern Cape that her home had never had a physcial address, it was a revelation. I simply did not comprehend what she was telling me. But when I encountered the Ndabakazi matter, it dawned on me that, decades after democracy, South Africa still did not belong to all who lived in it in a true sense of ownership.

It made no sense to me that the Ndabakazi community was erased and unseen, almost without any stake in the country. I was left wondering how many other rural communities across the country were denied the opportunity to assert themselves, where they live and have a say in how their land was used, because no effort has gone into surveying rural and former TBVC land. Moreover, the growth of the rural economy is impeded from meaningful development if no effort is made by government to secure land rights in the form of land surveying and securing the tenure of rural inhabitants.

This case exposed a tendency by corporations to regard traditional leaders as the automatic final arbiters and mouthpieces of the communities, without making legitimate attempts at engaging members of the those communities directly.

Chief Luzipho and the people of Ndabakazi were without any legal representation, and our asisstance to them was *pro bono*. Without an intentional and meaningful effort to enable and empower communities to access legal representation, the objective of pursuing social justice persists in its elusiveness. The people of Ndabakazi were unable to secure expert legal representation in the field of intellectual property, which required the services of a patent lawyer to advise and assist in the processes pertaining to the registration of the patent. With the latter not being our area of expertise, we needed to refer the matter to a specialist patent attorney. Patent lawyers are few and far in between. All recommended patent lawyers were already acting for other parties in the matter. The quest for justice for the people of Ndabakazi is ongoing.

40

Not a Black or White Issue

I was taken aback. For a change, this was not a consultation about a client looking to disinvest from land that was subject to a land claim or one who was nervous about the possibility of land being expropriated.

At this stage, my practice was typically characterised by two dominant, seemingly irreconcilable narratives: the client who is a landowner, a funder, a purchaser of land or an investor, often with deep pockets. In this world, it is easy to take for granted access to resources that enable ease of communication and well-resourced legal teams that ultimately lead to effective outcomes in resolving disputes. This is the world of the formal economy. It is also a world of formal language, clear deadlines and structure, where legal work has a level of predictability. Institutions such as courts and regulatory bodies were created as part of the world of commerce and the formal economy.

Diametrically opposed is a different world, one in which my

clients have no access to computers, data and offices. The rules, norms and standards that I seamlessly apply without batting an eyelid in Sandton are redundant in this world. I was not dealing with one, two or three contact people as the client. Here, I represent hundreds of members of communities based in far-flung rural areas across the provinces.

My legal skills became secondary. Meetings and engagements took place under trees, in community halls and on koppies overlooking the graves of ancestors. My reasonably eloquent siSwati, isiZulu, sePedi and isiXhosa skills became paramount. My team and I quickly learned to carry countless pens, notepads and a dictaphone on various trips. Few of the community members are literate. In this world, we could not schedule an hour or two for consultation. Community engagements often took a day or two. Instead of four or five signatures on a board resolution, we needed to ensure that we effectively secured hundreds of community signatures.

I was the same attorney having to service and assist people whose worlds would likely never collide. This is what I thought until I met Malcolm Segal.

Like me, Malcolm essentially believed in the moral and political need for land reform. We also shared the view that the state's role in land reform must go beyond simply awarding land to claimant communities. We believed that the future sustainability of the country and of land reform were inextricably linked to commerce and livelihoods. I was fortified in my view that capital and business had a stake and a role to play in ensuring that communities were not left in the same position they were in prior to the award of land to them.

Malcolm was an inspiring and long-standing entrepreneur. He wanted to explore the possibility of a long-term partnership with the Mdluli family, who were awarded land in the Kruger National Park but had no plans to ensure the land could be used for maximum value and for generations to come.

Malcolm had struck up a relationship with Chief Mdluli and his immediate family. He had engaged with the family for years with the assistance of the Commission on the Restitution of Land Rights. This culminated in a new company being formed, with members of the Mdluli Trust being parties and shareholders of the Mdluli Safari Lodge.

I saw the Mdluli matter as a blueprint of what was possible. Not only were the Mdluli people owners of 850 hectares of prime land in the Kruger, but they were also important players in tourism, conservation and pride in the land of their birth. The story of the victims of dispossession is turned on its head with the life-size bronze statue of the late Chief Mdluli greeting visitors from South Africa and abroad in the lodge's reception area, immortalising their story of triumph.

I saw myself as well placed. I was in a unique position. I understood the intricacies and pleas of communities in their need for land, the weakness in the laws and policies in practice, and the interests of capital and commerce. My role went beyond that of being an attorney. I became an enabler. It was paramount for me to turn fear into hope. I saw an opportunity for land reform to unite our divided past and to craft a narrative that is not dominated by conquest and bloodshed. Long after the land was awarded to the Mdlulis, they are not only owners of the land of their ancestors, they are also co-owners of a thriving safari lodge that attracts international and local tourists.

41

Changing Tides and a Shift in Land Politics

The country was experiencing weakened state institutions, diminished public trust and increasing unemployment. Cracks in the promise of a Rainbow Nation had emerged and the quest for an egalitarian society had slowed in the midst of claims of corruption.

My practice had grown exponentially in the firm, with large and complex cases that required more lawyers on my team, including junior directors, junior and senior associates and candidate attorneys. I was being entrusted with the mammoth responsibility of looking after the careers of younger lawyers. I saw this role as a way for me to give back for the years of grace and patience I had been gifted by my own mentors. I could open the doors for those lawyers who felt they were not worthy enough, and I could break down the walls of covert exclusion.

Beyond my land reform practice, my administrative and constitutional practice was thriving. I was in various courts representing entities that claimed the appointment of certain service providers was unlawful. Eskom's dilapidating infrastructure was a matter of public knowledge, with ageing power stations, a dwindling inability to guarantee power generation and supply, and incessant load-shedding.

The EFF had gained traction among the disgruntled youth, who felt a deep sense of discontent. Its campaign was centred on the nationalisation of land and expropriation of land without compensation. Illegal occupations were taking place on unserviced vacant land, on government-owned land and on private land. The EFF's approach to land had an immediate impact on the type of cases that landed on my desk. They mirrored the realities of societal power relations.

Legislation such as the Extension of Security of Tenure Act No. 62 of 1997 and the Prevention of Illegal Eviction from and Unlawful Occupation of Land Act No. 19 of 1998 were aimed at preventing people with insecure tenure rights, in rural and urban areas, from being evicted without a court order. These pieces of legislation are secondary laws that emanate from Section 25(7) of the Constitution. As the number of evictions escalated post-1994, the court's duty and judicial oversight increased to protect the rights of poor people. In many notable instances, the courts did not turn a blind eye to cases where eviction orders were sought to the detriment of the dignity of the downtrodden.

For the first time in its history, in December 2017, the ANC's 54th National Conference resolved to explore expropriation of land without compensation, without hampering food security and economic development. Two months later, the EFF tabled a motion in parliament to investigate the possibility of amending the Constitution to consider expropriation without compensation.

The historical and political significance of this momentous shift in the course of history was not lost on me. When the ANC came into power, it opted to pursue a land policy based on a willing-seller, willing-buyer policy. This was notwithstanding that the Constitution made provision for 'just and equitable' compensation, which arguably could be less than market value. The courts had tended to apply and favour market value as a means of compensation.

When the ANC voted in favour of the EFF motion in parliament in February 2018, I wondered whether the motion would linger longer than the ink drying on the resolution. My misgivings were based on the fact that the ANC and the EFF had vastly different ideological positions on their proposed land policies. The ANC policy was not based on disrupting or changing the land-ownership patterns that existed during apartheid, whereas the EFF's policy was based on the eradication of property rights, where land would be owned by the state and licensed out to citizens.

When it came to restitution, communities and families who were awarded land for restoration were left without any post-settlement support. And the backlog on the research and resolution of claims surpassed the speed at which they were being settled. I observed landowners' legal representatives pick holes in the legislation as they fobbed off claims based on legal technical arguments, with the assistance of historians who contended that the claimants voluntarily abandoned land and that they were not dispossessed as a result of past discriminatory laws. I noted how courts were faced with legal arguments that claimants did not form a 'community' as contemplated in the Restitution of Land Rights Act, and how hundreds of communities were expected to have homogeneous views about how they wanted to use the land after it had been restored. In the majority of cases where claimants opted for financial compensation, the policies that governed the amount of compensation only took into account market compensation and were devoid of losses that were intangible but equally significant, such as the sense of place, livestock, spiritual and cultural heritage, and a generational destruction of family units and family life.

My position on expropriation of land without compensation is that it has a legitimate place in our law and in the context of our history. I felt that there were instances where it could serve a genuine need, but I also held the view that it did not have the ability to solve all land reform issues. I was steadfast in my belief that I could play a part, however insignificant, in exploring the possibilities and solutions further.

42

Turning Points

I remember the feeling I had when I received the WhatsApp message inviting me to attend the GIBS Business School colloquium on land as a delegate. Apparently, my twelve years of involvement in the land reform arena as a black woman and attorney were not good enough to land me an automatic speaking slot at possibly the most attended and notable land colloquium. I was furious. I told the person organising the event that I was head of the Land Reform, Restitution and Tenure practice at one of the top five firms in the country, and I believed I had value to add to the conference as a speaker. When I looked down at my WhatsApp reply, I felt nauseous at having asserted myself in this way.

I am glad I did, because it was at this GIBS land colloquium in 2018 that I unleashed my full self: the girl from Meadowlands had come into her own.

I had prepared a speech on national land policy and legislative gaps in restitution, redistribution and land tenure. Aware of the gravity and importance of the opportunity to add my voice to the discourse, I was not going to hold back.

The moderator called me up to the stage. I took a deep breath as I scanned the more than 100-strong audience. I looked down at my notes and cue cards. I decided I was not going to rely on them. This moment called for me to speak from the heart – something that is counter-intuitive for a lawyer.

I began to speak about my personal journey, tracing it to 511K, through to school, university and ultimately law practice. Something intangible, spiritual and deeply personal was responsible for the words I was uttering. I spoke about the cases, the people and the challenges they had encountered. When I returned to my seat, the applause was so loud that I knew this moment was the genesis of something bigger than me.

As I walked out of the conference at the end, I was congratulated by senior ANC officials, who pulled me aside to enquire if I would be interested in attending the upcoming ANC Land Summit.

Two months later, I was afforded a slot at the ANC Land Summit to provide my views on whether or not the current Constitution made provision for expropriation without compensation.

The conference was filled to capacity. The atmosphere was abuzz with hope and promise, but it also had a sense of urgency. I appreciated being in the same space as respected intellectuals, academics, lawmakers and activists dedicated to exploring possible solutions to land reform.

I had decided I would bring to light the challenges of limited to no real land rights for the majority of poor people in South Africa. These were people living in informal settlements and backrooms in many townships. They were people whose names and addresses do not appear at the Deeds Office. These were poor people living in rural areas, often spoken for by traditional leaders, and with insecure land rights in the form of permissions to occupy. These were women, sisters, wives and girls who could be evicted from land as a result of patriarchal practices.

I outlined the plight of land claimants who were trapped in decision-making issues within trusts and Communal Property Associations. The CPAs are legal structures created by legislation that provides that once land claimants are awarded the land after a successful claim, they elect among themselves a leadership structure that takes decisions on how to regulate the use and possible investment of the land. In practice, communities often battle with in-fighting as a result of discord. In the context of land claims, communities invariably involve hundreds and thousands of people. The expectation that they must act as a homogeneous collective in making decisions is not only dangerous but it is also counter-intuitive. Many years in practice had taught me that the expectation placed on communities to act communally almost always resulted in years of unresolved litigation, broken families and sometimes even death.

I bemoaned the fact that although research and statistics had proven that over 80 per cent of South Africans were moving to cities and urban areas in pursuit of proximity to economic opportunities, our redistribution policies were heavily skewed in favour of farming, agriculture and rural occupation. When tracing the trajectory of the metamorphosis of these policies, I wondered why it was that there was still no legislation that informed South Africans who land was being awarded to, where the land was and the purpose for which it was being used.

It was the last day of the Land Summit and President Ramaphosa closed the conference. He did not speak for long, as we were told he had another engagement to attend. Seated next to me was a younger woman, clad in ANC regalia. We struck up a conversation, and she related to me how she intended to join the Johannesburg Bar after her part-time legal studies. As President Ramaphosa was being ushered out of the auditorium by his security cluster, the woman next to me, armed with youthful exuberance, looked in my direction, spontaneously grabbed my hand, and charged towards the president to take a selfie. Before I knew it, the president was stretching his hand out to greet me.

My lips moved faster than my brain. '*Mr President, it is a pleasure to meet you. My name is Bulelwa Mabasa, attorney, director and head of Land Reform, Restitution and Tenure at Werksmans Attorneys. I am delighted to have partcipated in the Land Summit. Please take my card. I am availing myself to assist and contribute my thoughts and experience. There is an urgent need to focus on this issue in a meaningful way.*'

The president's security team was becoming visibly agitated, signalling him to make his exit. Ignoring the pressure, the president looked into my eyes: '*I know who you are! I have followed and read your work. In fact, I saw your interview the other night on TV. I will be in touch. Thank you for your contribution!*'

He was then whisked away. I was indebted to my acquaintance for having nudged me to seize a moment that would change the trajectory of my life, of my career.

PART 6

A Duty to Serve

43

The Struggle for Land Justice

The day had come. The public announcement was made, and my mobile phone was abuzz with well-wishes from family, friends, colleagues and clients. The members of the Presidential Advisory Panel on Land Reform and Agriculture were named. My name was one of ten.

I received unreserved and overwhelming support from the firm and my partners. Adjustments were made to my annual budget, which freed me up to immerse myself in the work of the panel. Anele Ngidi had risen through the ranks and now anchored and directed my team.

We were invited to meet the president at his Mahlamba Ndlopfu official residence in Pretoria. I was accompanied on the drive by none other than Nani, who provided her usual guidance, protection and reassurance. It was reminiscent of us going to school in the cold winters, with our tiny bodies squeezed onto the torn back seat of an overcrowded taxi. But today was a comfortable drive in my Lexus, and Nani was in control of the music. The sounds of Ladysmith Black Mambazo carried us to our destination. We knew we were not driving alone. The rest of the car seats might have been empty, but there was no doubt in our minds that we were surrounded by Mawe, Tata, Ntate, Mme, Tale and Babam.

We were the first to arrive at the waiting area outside the boardroom. Minutes later, in walked Dr Vuyo Mahlati. I had not met her before. We introduced ourselves, and she was genial and engaging. Next to appear were Dan Kriek and Nick Serfontein, who both knew Vuyo well. I then met Thandi Ngcobo and instantly connected with her warm smile. I was pleasantly surprised to meet Thato Moagi and Wandile Sihlobo, both clearly younger than me but significant in the field of agriculture. Although I had been in various media interviews on land reform matters with Professor Ruth Hall and I was aware of her work, I had not personally met her before and I was struck by her gracious presence. With Professor Mohammad Karaan and Advocate Tembeka Ngcukaitobi, we constituted the Presidential Advisory Panel on Land Reform and Agriculture. We were an interesting and eclectic group – a combination of academics, historians, activists, commercial farmers, economists, an attorney and an advocate. This was a multidisciplinary and diverse team of professionals. The constitution of the members of the panel was clearly carefully considered. It was a microcosm of voices that I believe represented the interests of the country.

As chairperson of the panel, Vuyo opened each meeting by asking us to bow our heads in silence and be mindful of the magnanimity of the task we were called to undertake.

I had walked into the Union Buildings armed with my firmly

held positions. Soon into proceedings, I came to realise the complexities, nuances, realities and lived experiences of hundreds and thousands of South Africans, whom we had the gift of consulting with and learning from. This work was about forging a collective and unified perspective.

Over a period of eighteen months, the extensive engagements with direct and indirect stakeholders were eye-opening and sobering. My role required my ear and heart, more than it did my intellect and personal persuasions.

Many days and nights were dedicated to hearing stories from elderly women residing in rural KwaZulu-Natal, who told of their exclusion and arbitrary evictions from land in the absence of a son, husband or brother. These women related in isiZulu their lived reality of being denied access to land in the hands of traditional leaders. It was at the Rural Women Roundtable that I met the iconic land rights and gender activist Sizane Ngubane. From her life story, I began to comprehend the plight of poor African women who resided on communal land. I came to learn of the pervasive patriarchal practices that keep women as second-class citizens on decisions about land. This led to my suggestion that the panel should deal pointedly with the marginalisation of women in the context of land reform, which included a proposal on clear legislation that is aimed directly at favouring women as beneficiaries of redistribution programmes.

We also engaged widely with the National House of Traditional Leaders from all the provinces. My own convictions were challenged when I came across young men and women who were traditional leaders and bemoaned the lack of surveyed land, requesting assistance with geo-mapping and technological innovations. It was encouraging to encounter young traditional leaders who spoke vehemently against the practice of patriarchy within their own leadership structures. Many were open to the use of technological advancement to bring value and development to rural land. It was clear to me that the conversations about land and land reform were not taking place directly with those affected. What was espoused in newspapers was the normative narrative that all traditional leaders were dictatorial.

Through my law practice, I had often received queries and requests from landowners seeking clarity on the general land reform legal framework. As captains of industry, I earnestly felt that my clients should and must play a role and participate in finding solutions for the good of the country. This idea was sparked by the notion that land reform is not a concept that should interest only poor black people. I was of the view that our national psyche, identity and sense of social cohesion are directly linked to resolving the land question. I understood the coercive legal instruments involved in the expropriation of land, but I felt an opportunity existed to appeal to and provide a legal framework for those landowners who were able and willing to donate large tracts of land. While the law placed the legal obligation to deliver land reform on national government, I thought it would be a missed opportunity not to develop, formulate and introduce a land donations policy, enabling willing and able landowners to donate land for various uses. My proposal quickly found traction with the rest of the panel members.

From the workshops, seminars and engagements that were hosted at the firm with various players in government, business, banking institutions, non-profit organisations, land investors, academia and professional property bodies, it became abundantly clear to me that the tendency to overfocus on and place land reform within a rural and farming context resulted in the country not having the right conversations. For instance, the land reform question would not see meaningful resolution if discussions were not held about the role of capital, property developers, quantity surveyors and municipal officials in urban settings, where land was scarce and in demand. The dichotomous treatment of land reform, on the one hand, and property markets, on the other, needed to be linked in order to deal with the urban need for land.

In the panel's final report, I authored the sections on the identification, assessment and analysis of existing land legislation that was not fit for purpose. This legislation dissuaded land reform objectives and further perpetuated the apartheid legacy of dual citizenship, in terms of which the black majority living in informal settlements had no recognised land rights. I held this view because the ANC government passed legislation after 1994 that still today denies black people living in communal former TBVC states the autonomy and agency to assert legal rights in the form of legally recognised instruments such as lease agreements, title deeds and even mortgages. Equally, these laws have not been developed to enable registered titles for those in informal settlements. I proposed ways and means in which existing legislation should be developed and amended to enable the vast majority of black South Africans to finally have a legitimate stake in the land of their birth, by formalising their rights to land in a focused way.

As the panel delved deeper into the scourge of urban and rural evictions, I inevitably drew from the actual cases and matters that I was handling in my practice at the time. Although the legislation was in place in the form of the Extension of Security of Tenure Act (ESTA) and the Prevention of Illegal Eviction from and Unlawful Occupation of Land (PIE) Act, the Land Claims Court, Magistrate's Court and High Court were inundated with eviction cases in both urban and rural areas. Labour tenants, farm dwellers and unlawful occupiers were being evicted faster than their land rights were being upgraded. The debate within the panel was whether or not the time had come to put a moratorium on evictions. This idea did not come to pass, given that the Constitution provides for landowners to seek the court's sanction in the form of a court order before any person may be evicted. The jurisprudence of our courts insofar as evictions are concerned had developed to a point where courts themselves had to play an active, supervisory role in the context of the state's obligation to furnish alternative accommodation when an eviction order was granted.

In my practice, a mining company that had lawfully retrenched over 100 employees sought to evict the former mineworkers from leased premises that were secured and paid for by the mining company. Most of the former mineworkers were citizens of Lesotho and Mozambique and were recognised as 'occupiers' in terms of ESTA. My team and I represented the mining company seeking to evict the former mineworkers lawfully in terms of ESTA. The premises were being increasingly occupied by criminal elements, with people unrelated to the matter flocking to the area and unlawfully inviting others to the premises for gain. In no time, the mining company had lost control of the premises, and law enforcement agencies became overwhelmed and ill-equipped to provide law and order.

We assisted the mining company to issue notices to evict the former mineworkers, and ultimately a formal application was heard before the Land Claims Court. The court dismissed the mining company's application for eviction on the basis that the company should have first sought to terminate the former mineworkers' right of residence. By the time the court heard the matter, the former mineworkers had been in occupation of the premises for several years, and the mining company had incurred the cost of paying for the premises years after it was no longer receiving employment services from the former mineworkers.

It was taken to the Supreme Court of Appeal, and it was clear that the court sympathised with the plight and living conditions of the former mineworkers, such that the mining company was ordered to first terminate the former mineworkers' right of residence, thereafter to file notices to evict, and only then to file a formal application for eviction. These processes took over a year to complete, burdened by COVID-19, the lack of capacity in the Sheriff's Office and the inability of law enforcement agencies to assist in the safe service of the relevant notices at the premises. During COVID-19, a moratorium was placed on the execution of evictions during the national state of disaster. The conspectus of all these external issues meant that the mining company was left with the financial burden of continuing to pay for and provide premises for former mineworkers for a number of additional years. The legal wheels, which are notoriously known to be slow to turn, did not accelerate by any means. This case is one that exemplifies how courts are often compelled to come to the assistance of poor people involved in challenges that are often rooted outside the courtroom. The result is that lawyers and courts find themselves at the centre of disputes that appear to be legal in nature but are issues that stem from a state that is incapable of delivering on its mandate.

In the urban areas, the PIE Act mostly applies. Our team at the firm was approached by a listed property company based in Midrand, where parts of the land were unlawfully occupied by in excess of 100 people, who were engaged in waste picking and recyling activities. The occupiers settled in the middle of the office park adjacent to a sewer and created makeshift houses with cardboard and plastic. The vast majority of the occupiers were citizens of Lesotho, seeking to make a living. Assisting the landowner, we filed a formal eviction in the High Court in 2019. Almost three years later, the court had not granted the eviction order, given that the City of Johannesburg has not been able to provide alternative accommodation for the occupiers. In the interim, the property development company has had to bear the high cost of litigation, with no prospect of recovering its legal fees. In such cases, the existence of the Constitution as a guiding document for our society has little meaning in the context of a failing and incapacitated state that is unable to deliver on its service delivery imperatives.

In my practice, I received the most intriguing and first-of-its-kind case that would test the legality of a mayor's notice to expropriate vast pieces of land without compensation from my client, who was a property developer. My client wished to set aside the notice to expropriate the land in a review application before the court. Not only was the land being used for multiple purposes by our client, it also had existing schools and human settlements on it. The merits of this case were poor on the face of it. Expropriation is allowed in the Constitution where the landowner is not in current use of the property, where the landowner had not paid for land but rather received it as a state donation, and where there has not been any direct investment or improvements on the land made by the owner. In the case of my client, none of these requirements was satisfied.

I was left wondering how and why the mayor would have selected this particular case as a test case for expropriation when the law was so completely unfavourable to that set of circumstances. I was both disappointed and not surprised when the attorneys representing the mayor agreed to my client's order, leading to the setting aside of the notice to expropriate. To date, no cases have been brought to the courts to test the debate on whether or not Section 25 of the Constitution requires an amendment to enable expropriation without compensation.

My contribution to the panel on evictions was grounded on my lived experience not only as an attorney whose practice is dominated by those matters, but it was also influenced by my personal views and experience of having attended inspections of poor people's living conditions in squatter camps, on wetlands, on landslides and in landfills.

I authored the section in the panel report that deals with expropriation without compensation. I grounded this view on the need to understand and consider the fundamental principles underpinning the legal meaning of what constitutes 'property'. In essence, I was calling for a deliberation to develop current property legislation that would pointedly seek to resolve the absence of land tenure rights among the majority of landless people. I also observed that if the Constitution remained in its current form in Section 25, very few cases would enable the expropriation of land with zero compensation. In other words, expropriation without compensation had no prospect of delivering widescale, meaningful and sustainable land reform and land redistribution.

An important recommendation by the panel was the need to develop a single, national data portal for all land-related information in order to build a reliable and unified land administration system. We saw a dire need to fast-track the conclusion of restitution cases, such as the Nkosi case, and to create legal instruments of tenure for communities. Along with this, we recommended the review and refinement of landholding structures, such as Communal Property Associations and trusts. Churches, mining houses, municipalities, urban landlords, government, commercial farmers and agribusinesses would be encouraged to make land donations.

As the panel, we understood the importance of ascertaining land demand needs – where land was required, by whom and for what purposes. We recommended the strengthening of the Land Claims Court by ensuring that permanent judges are allocated to this court and we noted that the capacity of the Commission on the Restitution of Land Rights should be strengthened with additional skilled officials.

These were just some of the many recommendations made by the panel members. Each member worked tirelessly to produce a piece of work that has assisted in the development and review of the land reform question.

Looking back, I now realise that the most pertinent issues that

I felt the urgency to include in the work of the panel, which were previously not commonplace in the land reform debates, are being considered in various forums, including at academic institutions. The gift of playing a small part in the solution has not escaped me, and the beauty of it is seeing my work and ideas being taken forward in new policy-making by government and the Department of Agriculture, Land Reform and Rural Development.

Five months after the handing over of the panel's final report to the president and deputy president, I was approached by the Mapungubwe Institute for Strategic Reflection (MISTRA), which is directed and chaired by Joel Netshitenzhe. MISTRA planned to publish a book on land in South Africa, and I was being approached both as an experienced practitioner and also having played an instrumental role in the panel. I was invited to contribute my own chapter and co-edit the book with Khwezi Mabasa, an economist, consultant and academic. There was no blood relation, but I mischievously wondered if the ancestors of the family I had married into had conspired in this request. We worked together superbly. Initially, I felt inclined to decline the invitation, due to balancing the demands of the practice with my family life. It was clear I simply did not have the time. But I agreed. When COVID-19 hit and the hard lockdown was first introduced, not only was I engrossed in concerns about how the firm would approach the new world being thrust on us, but I had also placed myself in a position where I needed to drive the positioning of the book. In the end, Khwezi and I achieved our deadline to complete the manuscript.

While editing and writing *Land in South Africa: Contested Meanings and Nation Formation*, a dear friend of mine and a former colleague at Werksmans, Nompumelelo Seme, asked me to participate in an upcoming textbook by Wits academics on gender and the law. Mpumi managed to twist my rubber arm in a way only she can. She had left practice at Werksmans to join Wits University as a property law and tax lecturer. Before I knew it, amid COVID-induced home-schooling, with my house turned into a school by day and a place of work by night, I was drowning in textbooks, files, journals and studies in preparation for the chapter on gender and land reform.

The lessons, contributions and experience of having served on the panel remain etched in my heart and soul. Privileged and honoured to have served with intellectual giants, it remains my goal to take up the baton from the late Vuyo Mahlati and the late Mohammad Karaan. The fighting spirit of the late Sizane Ngubane is imprinted in my veins to continue the struggle for land justice in our lifetime.

44

An Ode to My Ancestors

All five of us – Bulelwa, Naniwe, Fuziswa, Ntombizone and Nomfundo – had seemingly come full circle after the loss of Tale and Babam, Mawe and Tata, Mme and Ntate. God, the universe, our angels and ancestors had granted us the peace, harmony, healing and closure that we so desperately yearned for. All of us had been graced with the gift of being merged with the loves of our lives.

Central to the marriage of one of my sisters that had taken place after our parents' passing was Siseko Nikelo. Siseko had been a constant presence in my childhood at 511K. His mischievous laughter entered the room long before his body did. He told us colourful stories about him and Babam carrying pangas in the violent 1980s for protection. Siseko's jovial character is not a reflection of an easy life. He had lost his wife and children in mysterious circumstances. According to him, it was a result of witchcraft and was caused by jealousy and envy.

We understood Siseko to be some kind of relative of Tata's from Zimbane in the Transkei, but we could never really stitch the relationship together. He grew up with Tata and migrated to Johannesburg, where he also lived at 511K with his wife. Like Tata, he too was an orphan who was looked after and raised by a circle of three families, neighbours and close-knit community members from Zimbane.

Remembering the role that Babam had afforded him in my traditional rites of passage and *lobola*, in the absence of my late parents, I felt a compulsion to bring him back from his retirement in Zimbane to lead my sister's nuptials as the only surviving elder. He openheartedly agreed to travel back to Johannesburg.

Two weeks after Nani's successful and blessed *lobola* negotiations, Siseko was still staying with me and Arthur. In between his love of watching golf, football and Formula 1, he was an avid lottery player and was never seen without what appeared to be a handwritten thesis on the probability of winning numbers on pages that must have been more than 40 years old. A welcome presence in our home, he represented to me the last piece of a puzzle and the only spiritual linkage to Tata's origins in Zimbane.

He was anxious to introduce me to Tata's lineage. Consumed by the urgency to complete this memoir, I did not take seriously his plot to get me to meet my grandmother who knew and grew up with Tata in Tata's adopted family.

'*Bullet, ndimfumene u Sis Mamazana. Uligqwetha. Ndifumene ne address yakhe.*' Not really taking in the content of his words, I half-heard and understood that what Siseko was insisting on was me meeting a long-lost grandmother I had not met, who, I am certain, he mistook to be a lawyer. What were the chances? I wondered if he was not experiencing early signs of dementia. He claimed that

AN ODE TO MY ANCESTORS

this grandmother lived fifteen minutes away from my house.

It was a crisp and cold afternoon on a Sunday, and I had been typing frantically on my laptop. Lured by the delicious aroma of roast chicken, I joined Arthur and Ntsumi in the kitchen, and exclaimed: '*I am almost done with the last chapter, but now Khulu Siseko insists I must meet this mysterious woman. I am thinking of postponing the visit to next week.*'

'No, my love, go. He has to have a valid reason why you must go.'

Before reversing the car out the garage, with Siseko in the passenger seat, I looked down at the address he had written on an unused lottery form. I punched the address into my GPS. We arrived at the gate. In front of us was a neatly kept suburban home, with an impressive rose garden. There was no response from the bell at the gate, so Siseko called the person he must have arranged this visit with.

'*Ndim lo Mkhele, vula ndise geytini.*' We were ushered in by a woman who cautiously welcomed us, her energy detached, and signalled for us to take a seat in the living room.

When the old lady entered the room, she gave us a wide smile, with an impressive set of pearly whites. She took a seat next to Siseko. It did not take long before they were reminiscing and laughing about people I had mostly never heard of.

When Siseko began to relate who I was, who my grandfather was – Nkwenkwe Elliott Khemese – her eyes sparkled. She related who her father was. H.R. Finca was a wealthy Methodist preacher, businessman and a generous community builder in Zimbane. She explained how in those days, people looked after each other. Blood relations paled into insignificance. No child was unclaimed. Tata and his sister Notizi were brought to the village after they were orphaned. They became the children of H.R. Finca, who took them on as adopted children. When Tata left the Transkei to work on the mines, his younger sister was guided through school and eventually studied to become a teacher, with the assistance and support of the Fincas.

'*Naye uligqwetha*,' Siseko said, pointing at me. The woman who opened the gate for us stood up and left the room. She came back carrying a photograph and an award, with the inscription: '*The Black Lawyers Association Honours Desiree Finca – The First Black Female Attorney in South Africa – Awarded on 8 April 2022.*'

I had goosebumps all over. On the Sunday before, I was certain I was ready to submit this manuscript of my memoir – on the eleventh anniversary of Tale's funeral, a day after we celebrated her brother Malome Mogotlha's 61st birthday and after I delivered a speech informing him of his influence in my chosen career as a lawyer. My ancestors were clearly not done with me yet.

In this room, at this moment, I met for the first time my 94-year-old grandmother, Desiree Mamazana Finca, born in 1928, and admitted as an attorney in 1967.

This signalled a journey of a thousand miles. The prayers answered and unanswered of multitudes of my ancestors, with dreams realised and dreams deferred. The voices and echoes seen and unseen. Known and unknown. In awe of the graciousness of the forces of those who came before me, I prayed for them to continue ordering my foosteps. A journey of a thousand miles is only but a beginning.

When Mama Phumla, who I found out was Makhulu Finca's

daughter, spontaneously gathered us around in a semi-circle and expressed gratitude and blessings for me, my husband and children, and the book I was writing, I knew. I knew that God had conspired to make this moment possible.

Tata's adopted younger brother Siseko had not only come to lead in Nani's *lobola* negotiations, he was also sent as a vessel. A bringer of hope.

'*You come from a long line of lawyers, attorneys and judges, my dear. This is who you are.*'

Acknowledgements

Being a practising lawyer for twenty years, I always took for granted my gift for writing. I found it to be an easy form of expression. I write opinions, briefs to counsel, client memoranda, letters to opponents, judges and colleagues, academic books and journals and the like almost daily. But none of that could have prepared me sufficiently for the kind of writing that calls for me as the subject. The process of writing my story has been cathartic, demanding, painful and joyous. This book allowed me to uncover a part of myself I was unaware of.

I am grateful to Eileen Bezemer, whom I 'met' virtually at my friend Wandile Sihlobo's book launch. She was the first person who thought of me as someone with an important story to tell. I salute her.

After Eileen, I was entrusted with a team of fabulous, understanding and insightful people at Pan Macmillan, who were truly amazing during the writing process. I must single out Andrea Nattrass for knowing exactly when to sympathise with my impossible schedule and when to firm up on deadlines.

ACKNOWLEDGEMENTS

One of the recurring themes of this book is the power of the invisible hand beyond talent, skill and expertise. This was my experience at the tail end of the book-editing process. As the last chapter was sent to me while I was travelling to New York with my sisters and husband, another gem landed. I found out that my editor on this book, Sally Hines, was also the editor of the book I co-edited entitled *Land in South Africa: Contested Meanings and Nation Formation*. It all made sense because Sally and I worked seamlessly together, and I am indebted to her for hearing my voice in the pages and for maintaining the essence of my writing.

I would like to acknowledge my firm and my co-partners and colleagues at Werksmans, whose legacy, imprint and influence run through my veins. I am blessed to be part of the Werksmans family that saw me join the firm as a 21-year-old woman 20 years ago. I am grateful for the grace shown to me in every endeavour and undertaking I have sought throughout my career.

A big thank you to my close circle of loyal and encouraging friends for their understanding throughout the writing of this work. I salute my lifelong sisterhood in Busi Dube and Mpho Boshego for their grace through cancelled dates and last-minute shifting of plans, and for journeying together since we were teenagers.

I remain grateful to my aunts, uncles and cousins from the Khemese and Mametse families for their unwavering support, reassurance and blessings in writing this memoir. I acknowledge the family I married into: the Mabasas and the Vilankulus. *Inkomu swinene!*

My sister-in-love, Caroline Mabasa, whispered in my ear many years ago that there was a story that was crying out to be told in the form of a book. My uncle, Moatisi Lehlongoane, urged me to consider documenting the story of the Khemese family. My friend and brother, Felipe Mazibuko, reiterated the validity and importance of my family's story. I thank my aunts, Mmane Happy Ndinisa and dadobawo Nonceba Ndhlovu, for furnishing me with old photographs of my grandparents.

My sisters – Naniwe, Fuziswa, Ntombizone and Nomfundo – you are everything that sisters should be and more. I treasure, respect, admire and love all of you so much. You all contributed to the making of this book. Each of your lives represents exactly who Tale and Babam were and are. I am nothing without you.

To all my children – Urhandzile Kurhula, Ntsumi Ntsako, Akani Rifumo and Harhi Rixaka Mabasa – you are perfect in every way. You cheered me on, asked how many words I had written on a daily basis, helped to read the book in its early stages and gave me wonderful suggestions. Thank you for making me want to be better and better. You are adored.

Last, but certainly not least, I salute my beloved husband Arthur, who is the rock, mentor and anchor in my life. He tolerated me typing away next to him in bed for hours on end. I treasure him for knowing and giving me exactly what I need at the right time. A gift from the ancestors – *Chauke! Xa humba!*

About the Author

Bulelwa Mabasa completed her studies at the University of the Witwatersrand in Johannesburg and was admitted as an attorney of the High Court in 2004. She started her legal career at Werksmans Attorneys, where she now occupies the position of director and head of the Land Reform, Restitution and Tenure practice. In August 2019, Bulelwa was named the 'Best Woman Lawyer in Land Rights' at the Women in Law (WOZA) awards ceremony. This was based not only on her contribution to Werksmans in this sector, but it also acknowledges the key role Bulelwa plays in land reform policy in South Africa, having been appointed by President Cyril Ramaphosa to the Presidential Advisory Panel on Land Reform and Agriculture in 2018. Her experience and written work, including as co-editor of *Land in South Africa: Contested Meanings and Nation Formation* (2021), has led to significant policy developments, and her suggestions have been carried through in the national sphere. Bulelwa has also contributed to major journals and publications on land reform, with a focus on gender.

www.ingramcontent.com/pod-product-compliance
Lightning Source LLC
Chambersburg PA
CBHW061936220426

43662CB00012B/1927